About Island Press

Island Press is the only nonprofit organization in the United States whose principal purpose is the publication of books on environmental issues and natural resource management. We provide solutions-oriented information to professionals, public officials, business and community leaders, and concerned citizens who are shaping responses to environmental problems.

In 1994, Island Press celebrated its tenth anniversary as the leading provider of timely and practical books that take a multidisciplinary approach to critical environmental concerns. Our growing list of titles reflects our commitment to bringing the best of an expanding body of literature to the environmental community throughout North America and the world.

Support for Island Press is provided by The Geraldine R. Dodge Foundation, The Energy Foundation, The Ford Foundation, The George Gund Foundation, William and Flora Hewlett Foundation, The John D. and Catherine T. MacArthur Foundation, The Andrew W. Mellon Foundation, The Joyce Mertz-Gilmore Foundation, The New-Land Foundation, The Pew Charitable Trusts, The Rockefeller Brothers Fund, The Tides Foundation, Turner Foundation, Inc., The Rockefeller Philanthropic Collaborative, Inc., and individual donors.

The Freshwater Imperative

The Freshwater Imperative

A RESEARCH AGENDA

Edited by Robert J. Naiman,
John J. Magnuson,
Diane M. McKnight,
Jack A. Stanford,
and other members of
the FWI Steering Committee

ISLAND PRESS
Washington, D.C. · Covelo, California

Library of Congress Cataloging in Publication Data
The freshwater imperative : a research agenda / edited by Robert J.
  Naiman . . . [et al.].
      p.   cm.
    Includes bibliographical references (p.   ) and index.
    ISBN 1-55963-406-5 (cloth : acid-free paper).—ISBN
  1-55963-407-3 (paper : acid-free paper)
      1. Limnology—Research.   2. Ecosystem management—Research.
  3. Water quality management—Research.   I. Naiman, Robert J.
  QH96.5.F74   1995
  574.5'2632'072—dc20   94-39852
                                                                   CIP

Contents

Figures, Tables, and Boxes

Figures

Tables

Boxes

Foreword

Virtually every view of our planet from orbit reminds one that we live on a water planet, for Earth's hydrosphere presents an endless variety of awe-inspiring scenes. Naturally, one first notices the grand expanses, the myriad islands, and the overwhelming vastness of our saline oceans. But the freshwater components of our hydrosphere are also spectacular in their size and diversity. Clouds are abundant, sometimes predominant, on any given revolution around the planet; snows drape the immense mountain ranges and blanket enormous continental plains; stark white ice covers Greenland, the Arctic, and the Antarctic, and the adjacent oceans are dotted with floes and bergs of varying size; great lakes fill major geologic features in North America (Great Slave, Great Bear, the five "Great Lakes"), Africa (Tanganyika, Malawi), and Asia (Baikal); the moon's reflection races along with the spacecraft during a nighttime pass, revealing the course of one of the world's great rivers and the extent of surrounding marshlands as it glances and glitters off the waters. The immensity, intricacy, and beauty of our hydrosphere are impressive indeed.

But both history and current resource statistics tell us that this appearance of enormity is a dangerous illusion. A recent summary of key water statistics in the September/October 1994 issue of *International Wildlife* points out that only some three percent of all the water on this fluid planet of ours is fresh water. Of this, nearly 75 percent is locked up in ice caps and glaciers, and much of the rest is stored in underground aquifers. When it comes to meeting humanity's water needs, we have ready access via surface sources to only some 14 percent of the planet's fresh water. Since this quantity does not grow in proportion to the Earth's population increases, our global water supply is stretching increasingly thin. The United Nations calculates that the per capita amount of available fresh water has shrunk by roughly a factor of four from 1850 to 1993. Yet water demand is projected to double in over half the world's countries by the year 2000. Writing in *Poor Richard's Almanac* in 1733, Benjamin Franklin observed, "When the well's dry, we know the worth of water." Are we on the way to experiencing the truth of his observation?

The contributors to this volume have been ahead of their time in recognizing the growing importance of freshwater issues to humankind in general and to the United States in particular. They have set out to establish a research framework that links key natural phenomena, processes, scales, and concepts into a coherent whole. They address the need to bring together the too-often separated insights, questions, and information requirements of scientists, resource managers, and the public, and also to link the biophysical and socioeconomic dimensions of critical water issues. Two key attributes of this approach are the primacy of regional scale efforts and the clear recognition that the development of predictive capabilities is essential if we are ever to cope successfully with unforeseen events, or to develop what today are called "adaptive" management regimes. Another indication of the prescience of the contributors is found in the fact that, as this book goes to print, concepts such as these are just beginning to figure explicitly in federal science policy and program planning.

The authors also point out that the amount of national water expenditures devoted to understanding the biophysical and socioeconomic aspects of our freshwater resources is proportionately very small—$500 million or less out of $50 billion in total annual water-related expenditures. By clearly displaying the number and complexity of freshwater research challenges we face, they make a strong case for the need to increase current efforts. Regardless of the amount available, the paramount importance of water to all life on this planet makes it necessary that we spend this sum wisely, so that "the worth of water" becomes clearer to society and we are better equipped to be wise stewards of our freshwater resources. *The Freshwater Imperative* provides us with a sound framework by which to do this.

Kathryn D. Sullivan
Chief Scientist, National Oceanic and Atmospheric Administration
Former Astronaut

Preface

The Freshwater Imperative (FWI) workshop and this ensuing book resulted from a proposal presented by Robert J. Naiman and John J. Magnuson in 1991 to the National Science Foundation (NSF grant no. DEB-9207824). The purpose was to identify research opportunities and frontiers in inland water ecology for this decade and beyond—that is, to develop a research agenda for limnology. The workshop and ensuing activities were funded in 1992 by the NSF and four other agencies: the Environmental Protection Agency (EPA), the National Aeronautics and Space Administration (NASA), the National Oceanic and Atmospheric Administration (NOAA), and the Tennessee Valley Authority (TVA).

The catalyst for the Freshwater Imperative came from an ad hoc group of individuals in U.S. federal agencies who were interested in fresh water and concerned about the need to develop a foundation for responsible care and management of inland waters. In the late winter and spring of 1990 they developed a charter for the FWI, at that time called the Freshwater Initiative. The essence of that charter persists through the present document. The goal was to acquire a *predictive* understanding of freshwater ecosystems and resources that can be used to improve detection, assessment, and forecasting of environmental effects and to develop management and mitigation alternatives for scenarios of potential environmental change. From the beginning, the interagency FWI group sought review and input from the scientific community by sending its initial defining document to sixty aquatic scientists for comment.

This interagency FWI group first met in April 1990 to form the FWI Coordinating Council. By January 1991 membership included individuals from the Departments of Agriculture (DOA); Commerce (DOC), Energy (DOE), and the Interior (DOI) and from the EPA, the TVA, NASA, the NSF, and the U.S. Army Corps of Engineers (ACE). The Coordinating Council was chaired first by Maurice Averner (NASA) and then by Penelope L. Firth (NSF). The Council continues to meet every few months and is currently assessing decision makers' needs in the freshwater sciences.

The workshop and process reported on here to develop a research agenda was planned and cochaired by Robert J. Naiman and John J. Magnuson, with the assistance of a Steering Committee broadly based in freshwater sciences. Members of the Steering Committee were G. Ronnie Best, University of Florida; Elizabeth R. Blood, University of South Carolina, now at the Joseph W. Jones Ecological Research Center; Nelson G. Hairston Jr., Cornell University; Gene E. Likens, Institute of Ecosystem Studies; Sally MacIntyre, University of California; Diane M. McKnight, U.S. Geological Survey; Jeffrey E. Richey, University of Washington; Jack A. Stanford, University of Montana; and Robert G. Wetzel, University of Alabama. Penelope L. Firth participated in Steering Committee meetings as an observer for the National Science Foundation and as liaison to the FWI Coordinating Council. The committee met three times: in July and November 1992 and in December 1993.

The principal workshop was held on 10–15 January 1993 at the University of Washington Marine Laboratory at Friday Harbor, Washington. The thirty-six participants (in addition to Steering Committee members) included scientists from twenty-five U.S. research institutions and professional organizations, six foreign institutions, and five federal agencies (participants are listed in appendix 1). The philosophy of the Steering Committee has been to keep the process open and to encourage debate within an atmosphere of respect. This was certainly the tone of the workshop and the ensuing presentations at national professional meetings and during preparation of the recommendations. The Steering Committee was also sensitive to the potential for professional conflicts and from the beginning included all aspects of limnology, freshwater ecology, and inland water ecology in its charge.

The openness of the process has been, and continues to be, a high priority. Prior to the workshop, short articles on the FWI process were placed in newsletters of scientific societies having members with strong interests in aquatic sciences, and responses were sought on their ideas for the research agenda. Following the Friday Harbor workshop, discussion of the FWI recommendations was placed on the programs of major scientific and professional societies related to freshwater ecology. The draft Executive Summary of the FWI was presented and comments were received. By March 1994, the Steering Committee had made presentations and sought comments at annual meetings of the American Fisheries Society, the American Society of Limnology and Oceanography, the Ecological Society of America, the International Association of Great Lakes Research, the North American Benthological Society, the Society of Wetland Scientists, the Hydrology Section of the American Geophysical Union, and the North American Lake Management Society.

During the Friday Harbor workshop, drafts of the initial ideas were proposed by Allen P. Covich, Colorado State University; Clifford N. Dahm,

University of New Mexico; Stuart G. Fisher, Arizona State University; Paul Hebert, University of Guelph; Robert W. Howarth, Cornell University; James R. Karr, University of Washington; James F. Kitchell, University of Wisconsin; John J. Magnuson; G. Richard Marzolf, U.S. Geological Survey; Diane M. McKnight; Judy L. Meyer, University of Georgia; John C. Morse, Clemson University; Robert J. Naiman; Michael L. Pace, Institute of Ecosystem Studies; Michael M. Pollock, University of Washington; and Jack A. Stanford.

Following the Friday Harbor workshop, a first draft document was prepared by Robert J. Naiman and added to by Penelope L. Firth, John J. Magnuson, and Diane M. McKnight. It was then reviewed by the entire Steering Committee before being sent to all workshop participants for comment and further changes. This document represents a consensus of participants at the workshop with extensive input from the limnological community at large. Where necessary we have dealt with differences of opinion by recognizing or including both views or making difficult choices when we felt we must.

The final version of the FWI research agenda has been endorsed by the following professional organizations: the American Society of Limnology and Oceanography, the Association of Ecosystem Research Centers, the Ecological Society of America, the International Association for Great Lakes Research, the North American Benthological Society, the North American Lake Management Society, and the Society of Wetland Scientists.

Preparation of this book and formation of the final recommendations benefited greatly from comments by Arthur E. Bogan, Carnegie Museum of Natural History; Stephen R. Carpenter, University of Wisconsin; William Chang, NSF; George D. Constantz, Pine Cabin River Ecological Laboratory; Colbert E. Cushing, Battelle-Pacific Laboratory; David Dow, NOAA; Paul Hebert, University of Guelph; David Klarer, Ohio Department of Natural Resources; Gary G. Mittelbach, Michigan State University; Russell Moll, NSF; Karen Porter, University of Georgia; Michael Quigley, Great Lakes Environmental Research Laboratory; Al Rango, DOA; Janet W. Reid, National Museum of Natural History; David W. Schindler, University of Alberta; Robert W. Sterner, University of Texas; Fred N. Swader, DOA; Camm C. Swift, Los Angeles County Museum of Natural History; Alan J. Tessier, Michigan State University; and William Waldrop, TVA. We thank the people who helped in the publication of the book, including Pat Harris for her commendable copyediting, and Barbara Youngblood of Island Press.

We also thank the following persons, who were most helpful in preparing the proposal, planning and conducting the workshop, and preparing the manuscript: University of Washington—Ms. Carla A. Manning, Mr. Michael M. Pollock, Ms. Jennifer R. Sampson, and Dr. G. Lee Link of the Center for Streamside Studies; Mr. Kenneth J. Bible and Ms. Kathryn A. Kohm of the Olympic Natural Resources Center. University of Wisconsin-Madison—Ms. Elizabeth A. Krug of the Center for Limnology and Ms. Eulah Sheffield, for the design of our workshop memento of waters from Lake Mendota, Lac Léman, Okefenokee Swamp, Hubbard Brook, and the Colorado River, which symbolize the historical roots and breadth of limnology.

Robert J. Naiman

John J. Magnuson

Diane M. McKnight

Jack A. Stanford

The Freshwater Imperative

Executive Summary

Fresh Water and Society

Fresh water is a strategic resource in a rapidly changing world. It is a source of energy, an avenue of transportation, habitat for a myriad of organisms, and essential for life. Fresh water structures the physical landscape, is a central feature of climate, and greatly influences economic growth and demographic patterns. Yet as the human population increases, more and more demands are placed on freshwater ecosystems. Already, sufficient clean water and healthy aquatic habitats have become a rare natural resource. Understanding the abilities of freshwater ecosystems to respond to human-generated pressures and their limitations in adapting to such challenges has become vital to long-term societal stability. These are problems for basic science, they reflect national and global needs, and they must be addressed now.

Scientists and managers are increasingly called on to provide a predictive understanding of freshwater ecological systems but are unable to respond effectively at a scale commensurate with the issues. There are two primary reasons for this. First, funding and infrastructure for freshwater sciences have dwindled while U.S. government agencies expend enormous resources on ineffective management activities that have a poor scientific foundation. The Freshwater Imperative seeks management strategies that are more efficient and less costly in the long term. To achieve these goals, management and science must be balanced and integrated more effectively. Second, the current dependence on short-term studies does not allow separation of human-caused changes from natural environmental change. As a result, unambiguous criteria for management and policy decisions are generally lacking.

Changes in the distribution, abundance, and quality of water and freshwater resources in this century represent a strategic threat to the quality of human life, the environmental sustainability of the biosphere, and the viability of human cultures. The United States is facing, in a real sense, a freshwater imperative. Will freshwater sciences and management be ready, as professions, to meet this challenge?

1

Why Freshwater Sciences and Management?

Limnology—freshwater sciences and management—is dedicated to understanding inland lakes, reservoirs, rivers, streams, wetlands, and groundwater as ecological systems. The field is inherently multidisciplinary, involving all viewpoints that can be brought to bear on understanding the nature of fresh waters (Edmondson 1994). As demands for freshwater resources increase, resource managers and policy makers must ensure that the benefits from water use and the protection of water resources are optimized. The United States spends approximately $50 billion annually to protect aquatic systems; wise use of these funds requires a comprehensive and integrated understanding of those ecosystems (Environ- mental Protection Agency 1991; National Research Council 1992). This requirement underlies the integrating theme of the Freshwater Imperative (FWI) research agenda: providing a predictive understanding of inland aquatic systems in a changing world.

Recently a number of deficiencies have been identified in our national infrastructure supporting freshwater sciences. They include the inability to predict the future vitality of altered environments, to combine environmental and socioeconomic sciences into an integrated ecosystem perspective, and to provide a national research and education framework that allows an effective response to emerging issues. These deficiencies are related to (1) the fact that less than 20 percent of the $2.5 billion in federal funds expended annually on environmental research and development goes toward basic research in ecology (Gramp, Tpich, and Nelson 1992) and (2) the difficulties of integrating scientific disciplines and coordinating management among varying agency mandates.

Against this background, the National Science Foundation (NSF), the Environmental Protection Agency (EPA), the National Atmospheric and Space Administration (NASA), the Tennessee Valley Authority (TVA), and the National Oceanographic and Atmospheric Administration (NOAA) sponsored a working group of leading aquatic scientists to identify research opportunities and frontiers in freshwater sciences for the 1990s and beyond. This book summarizes that two-year effort. The following Freshwater Imperative research agenda is framed by science issues with immediate policy relevance and by fundamental research to help ensure that today's uncertainties do not become tomorrow's problems.

Determinants of Research Priorities

Research priorities need to address the following national issues related to freshwater ecosystems that affect the long-term vitality of human societies and the biosphere: (1) freshwater ecosystems play a central role in balancing socioeconomic values and environmental sustainability; and (2) the scope of water-related environmental issues (ecological impoverishment, water availability, and human health and quality of life) exceeds the capacity of individual disciplines, institutions, or nations to address them.

These issues exist at regional as well as national and global scales. Because research and management are most effective at the regional scale, the FWI identifies regional objectives that address (1) prediction of the effects of regional climate and landscape change on freshwater ecosystems; (2) development of an environmental perspective from which biophysical and socioeconomic scientists can work cooperatively toward an understanding of regional aquatic problems; and (3) resolution of regional freshwater problems through an understanding of underlying systemic factors.

Each of these regional objectives is closely related to the others. By emphasizing prediction of change at the regional scale, the FWI seeks to encourage diverse political and institutional cooperation, to develop broader environmental perspectives and approaches, and to resolve issues at geographic scales relevant to human communities. An integrated regional socioeconomic-ecological perspective requires institutional and interdisciplinary cooperation at a level seldom achieved in the past but of absolute necessity for the future. The nation's freshwater scientists and managers must assume a leading role in developing a holistic understanding of fundamental factors underlying freshwater problems and issues. Effective managerial solutions to problems concerning freshwater resources will be achieved only with explicit recognition that changes in environmental conditions are directly linked to socioeconomic patterns and processes.

Collectively, these national water issues and regional-scale objectives raise a number of fundamental questions about integrating freshwater research priorities with human needs: (1) How can we predict regional environmental change resulting from alterations in the hydrologic regime? (2) How can we better understand linkages between human activities and the maintenance of viable biotic communities? (3) How should we develop measures for reliable evaluation of human influences on freshwater ecosystems over broad spatial and temporal scales? And (4) how can we provide a scientific infrastructure that allows an effective response to emerging issues? Addressing these integrating questions (table E.1) together with regional objectives (figure E.1), and making managerial and policy decisions based on the answers to those questions, is fundamental to sustaining the nation's societies and freshwater ecosystems.

Table E.1 Questions Integrating Freshwater Research Challenges with Human Needs

1. Predicting regional change in freshwater ecosystems: What are the ecological effects of changes in the amount and routing of water and waterborne materials along the hydrologic flow path, from precipitation to the ocean, under natural and altered conditions?

2. Evaluating human effects on freshwater systems: What are the effects of human activities on aquatic communities, and how do they influence the sustainability of freshwater resources?

3. Identifying aquatic indicators: Are there key features of freshwater ecosystems that can be used to evaluate and predict the effects of human influences on regional to continental scales?

4. Resolving emerging freshwater issues: What research infrastructure is necessary to provide effective responses to issues not yet perceived or elaborated?

The Freshwater Imperative (FWI) Research Agenda

The regional objectives and integrating questions outlined in the previous section are the foundation for the FWI research agenda. The agenda focuses on three water issues of fundamental importance to the United States: water availability, aquatic ecosystem integrity, and human health and safety. The research agenda addresses scientific issues that relate directly to the needs of society, predictive management of freshwater resources, and the ability to meet future needs as unforeseen freshwater issues emerge.

Even though the final conclusions and recommendations of the FWI research agenda are themselves the work of a diverse group of freshwater scientists, they were circulated among a number of professional organizations to verify that the agenda's elements indeed reflect (as much as is possible) a consensus among freshwater scientists. Subsequently, several organizations have endorsed the FWI: the American Society of Limnology and Oceanography, the Association of Ecosystem Research Centers, the Ecological Society of America, the International Association for Great Lakes Research, the North American Benthological Society, the North American Lake Management Society, and the Society of Wetland Scientists.

Each of the following priority research areas is integrative and incorporates elements that are scientifically significant and socially relevant; each seeks predictive understanding of freshwater ecosystems and resources at the regional scale for the long term, and each encourages development of new paradigms in freshwater science and management.

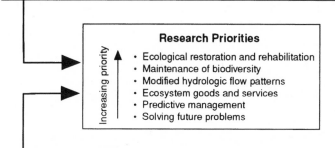

National Water Issues

- Freshwater ecosystems are the central component of regional and global sustainability
- Cooperation is required to address
  — Ecological impoverishment
  — Water availability
  — Human health and quality of life

Regional Objectives

- Predicting regional-scale change
- Sustaining socioeconomic and environmental integrity
- Resolving systemic issues

Integrating Questions

- Predicting change in systems
- Evaluating human effects on systems
- Identifying aquatic indicators
- Resolving emerging issues

Research Priorities

Increasing priority

- Ecological restoration and rehabilitation
- Maintenance of biodiversity
- Modified hydrologic flow patterns
- Ecosystem goods and services
- Predictive management
- Solving future problems

Research Infrastructure

CENTERS
- Freshwater Biodiversity
- Regional Analysis
- Technology Development and Transfer
- Limnological Synthesis and Analysis

RESEARCH SITES
- Additional long-term unimpaired sites
- Long-term toxic or altered sites
- Enhancement of existing sites

EDUCATION AND COMMUNICATION
- Basic academic training and individual research
- Training grants
- Professional education

Institutional Support

NATIONAL SCIENCE FOUNDATION
- Cooperative interdisciplinary program

INTERAGENCY EFFORTS
- Collaborative interagency program patterned on ad hoc FWI group

REGIONAL INSTITUTIONS
- Cooperation among federal and state agencies, universities, and private sector

EXISTING FRESHWATER PROGRAMS
- Enhancement through budgetary and infrastructural development

Figure E.1 Freshwater Imperative (FWI) Research Priority Framework

Scientific Issues

The FWI research agenda supports research on four scientific issues related directly to the needs of human society: restoring and rehabilitating ecosystems, maintaining biodiversity, understanding the effects of modified hydrologic flow patterns, and describing the importance of ecosystem

Table E.2 Fundamental Freshwater Research Issues with Direct Consequences for Human Society

Definition	Forcing Functions	Effects of Forcing Functions	Key Research Needs
Ecological Restoration and Rehabilitation			
Reconstruction of systems that have lost ecological functions supporting natural regimes of productivity, biogeochemical-cycling, and evolution	Habitat destruction, alteration, fragmentation, and defragmentation. Pollution effects. Introduction of exotic species. Acid deposition	Loss of biological resources, ecological integrity, self-purification capacity, system productivity, and resilience and resistance to disturbance. System simplification	Application of basic principles of biophysical sciences to aquatic resource restoration. Aquatic resource management (habitat, systematics, effects of exotics); assessment of aquatic resources (habitat and ecological diversity). Role of disturbance regimes; microbial processes and linked biogeochemical cycles. Studies of land-water ecotones
Maintenance of Biodiversity			
Maintenance of the totality of life on earth, in all its variety of molecular, genetic, taxonomic, ecological and landscape patterns	Habitat destruction, alteration, and fragmentation and defragmentation. Pollution effects	Loss of "biological warehouse." Diminished resilience and resistance to disturbance. System simplification. Loss of ecological integrity	Development of innovative technology for systematic and evolutionary biology. Effects of individual species on ecological processes. National biodiversity inventory. Genotypic variation. Control of speciation and phenotypic variation
Modified Hydrologic Flow Regimes			
Changes in routing of water and materials along the hydrologic flow path from precipitation to	Altered landscapes, wetlands, streams, rivers, lakes, and groundwater systems.	Changes in amount, timing, and routing of water (and the life and materials in it) along	Integration of land use policy with aquatic system sustainability. Integration of aquatic ecological engineering

the ocean	Desertification. Global climate change	the hydrologic flow path. Ecological impoverishment and sedimentation. Loss of ecological goods and services. Habitat destruction. Loss of connectivity among ecological components	into surface water management. Effects of environmental change on the flux of organisms, sediments, organic matter and nutrients through inland waters. Effects and feedbacks between biotic communities and material fluxes. Influences of landscape alterations on material and toxic fluxes. Biophysical interactions
Ecosystem Goods and Services Provision for viable ecological communities while meeting the needs of the present without compromising the integrity of resources to future generations	Pollution. Altered demographic conditions. Intergenerational environmental knowledge. Institutional regulations. Market forces	Degraded drinking water quality. Contamination of aquatic foods. Transmittal of infectious diseases. Declining renewable resource base. Irreversible environmental degradation	Studies of multiple-insult, cumulative effects. Understanding of indirect effects of institutional decisions. Role of aesthetics and recreation in human health. Economic and social consequences of impaired ecological services. Development of conservation strategies

goods and services provided by freshwater ecosystems. Each involves the effects of accelerated, largely anthropogenic regional environmental change (table E.2).

Predictive Management

The FWI research agenda recommends that management of the nation's freshwater ecosystems be founded on integrative and accurate measures of human and environmental conditions. The FWI research agenda recognizes the need to provide predictive tools and innovative managerial approaches now and in the future. This research issue is so broad and of such contemporary importance that it has been divided into four subcomponents: disturbance regimes, physical and biological legacies, integrative ecological properties, and model development (table E.3). The agenda encourages intensified research toward the development of new paradigms of freshwater science and management.

Solution of Future Problems

The FWI research agenda recognizes that interdisciplinary and investigator-initiated basic research programs have been an outstanding and proven investment in the nation's capability to detect and solve previously unrecognized problems (table E.4). Scientists conducting basic research and managers exploring innovative solutions are of primary importance in coping with unforeseen problems associated with freshwater ecosystems. The FWI research agenda recommends the development and maintenance of a national scientific infrastructure that can be effective in addressing emerging issues.

Linking Research, Management, and Policy

Proactive and continuous interaction between freshwater research and government agencies with various management mandates is vital to developing and implementing a progressive national water policy. Moreover, research must effectively interact with management and policy-making processes over short time frames and in terms understood by the nation's citizens. The FWI research agenda encourages an adaptive management approach (Lee 1993), recognizing that the urgency and scale of freshwater issues require that many management and policy decisions be made now. Given the inherent uncertainties, large-scale restoration and management projects are best viewed as experiments with mechanisms for regular assessment and adaptive change to produce an ever-improving

Table E.3   Measurements of Human and Environmental Conditions That Build
the Foundation for Freshwater Ecosystem Management

Definition	Key Research Needs
Disturbance Regimes	
Patterns of recurring, discrete events that significantly alter biological and physical characteristics of a biotic community or system	• Identifying historical disturbance regimes • Understanding biotic effects and responses to historical disturbances (paleolimnology, genetic legacies) • Integrating biotic and physical sciences • Understanding the role of animals in influencing system-level processes
Physical and Biological Legacies	
The physical remnant, or "signature," of a past biophysical event that profoundly influences the condition of the system at various times into the future	• Identifying origins and historical spatio-temporal development patterns of past, present, and future legacies • Understanding the role of legacies in ecosystem function • Understanding current and projected patterns of legacy development
Integrative Ecological Properties	
Ecological characteristics that reveal the states of human and environmental systems by integrating specific processes across spatial and temporal scales	• Understanding accumulated insults and influences • Identifying key biotic and biogeochemical markers • Developing sophisticated modeling approaches on regional scales
Model Development	
Forecasting of changes in freshwater ecosystems driven by management, human-induced stress, and environmental change	• Improving the overall knowledge base • Advancing modeling approaches • Creating the capacity to predict responses to environmental change for a wide variety of ecosystems and stresses and to forecast over broad spatial and temporal scales • Undertaking long-term studies and developing mechanisms for collaboration, data sharing, and transdisciplinary synthesis

product. To do this, managers and policy makers must invest in research, and scientists must be cognizant of the information needs of managers and policy makers. Three themes are of high priority: (1) evaluation of "best management practices," (2) application of ecological engineering techniques, and (3) monitoring and assessment (table E.5). The FWI proposes

Table E.4 Developing the Nation's Infrastructure
for Freshwater Science and Management

Definition	Key Research Needs
Solving Future Problems	
Preparing an infrastructure that will be responsive to unforeseen and emerging freshwater issues	• Setting priority needs from interdisciplinary and investigator-initiated research and management programs • Creating new approaches to regional analyses and development of complex modeling regimes

a model, based on the reorganization of Department of the Interior research personnel in the National Biological Service (NBS), to uniquely link research, management, and policy as it affects freshwater resources.

Implementation Requirements

Implementation of the FWI priority research areas and their integration with management and policy involves changes in institutions as well as improvements in infrastructure. Actions recommended in this book demand administrative leadership to ensure that an adequate base of information and expertise is available as the nation faces water-related threats to its quality of life and the sustainability of the environment and human culture. The centerpiece of the implementation strategy is a coordinated interagency initiative with private sector partnerships that draw on the expertise of agency scientists and managers, academic researchers, and private sector groups. The FWI does not duplicate successful ongoing activities. Rather, it provides a framework for coordination among agencies and between federal and nonfederal partners. It emphasizes connections between scientists and decision makers as well as issue-focused research. The proposed research will build a better scientific understanding of freshwater systems for the future, and address current research needs related to the specific missions of government agencies in a coordinated and efficient manner.

As freshwater science scales up to a regional, longer-term focus, there are several general recommendations for maintaining and enhancing the intellectual and technical vigor of the discipline. These include: ensuring continuance of long-term studies; including social and economic models in ecological studies; augmenting data acquisition at long-term monitoring sites to include experimental and modeling components; organizing

Table E.5 Research Directed Toward Effectively Integrating the
FWI Research Directions with Management and Policy

Definition	Key Research Needs
Linking Research, Management, and Policy	
Making informed decisions and taking effective actions to ensure the well-being of freshwater resources for present and future generations	• Critical evaluation of "best management practices" with respect to land and water use • Development and application of innovative ecological engineering techniques to mitigate human-caused degradation of water and aquatic habitat • Application of statistically valid approaches to regional monitoring and assessment

efforts to interface with sites outside the United States to produce a global perspective; expanding the applicability of general ecological principles; and coordinating with the Center for Environmental Analysis and Synthesis for enhanced synthesis of data, models and concepts derived from regional sites.

The Freshwater Imperative should be continually refined as new knowledge becomes available, and as emerging freshwater issues demand responses. As the FWI matures into a research program, it will require sustained effort to maintain vision, accountability, and external evaluation.

Implementation of the FWI research program is expected to cost approximately $200 million per year—less than 1 percent of what the United States spends annually on procurement, regulation, and remedial protection of its waters. It is the considered opinion of the FWI Steering Committee and the professional societies supporting the FWI (see page 4) that the FWI research agenda is timely, balanced, and relevant and that its costs are thoroughly justified and appropriate. The Freshwater Imperative will move the U.S. toward development of predictive understanding and world-class expertise on strategic issues that have both local importance and global significance. The proposed program will encourage more effective leveraging of scarce fiscal resources toward addressing environmental and socioeconomic problems. It will also improve policy and management decision-making directed toward the environmental sustainability of inland waters. Finally, the Freshwater Imperative will promote fundamental advances in knowledge to support informed responses to future problems.

Many agencies are moving toward an ecosystem management approach. The FWI supports this movement and encourages the incorporation into agency programs of an integrated watershed management perspective.

Key elements of this approach are a science-management-policy partnership, increased resources for extramural research, and freshwater scientific advisory panels for agency directors. The estimated cost of $20 million per year would provide more effective water management, including anticipation and resolution of critical environmental problems.

Institutional support for the FWI can be provided by the following:

- Enhancing existing programs of government agencies with water resource responsibilities to support innovative research and technology development and transfer. Key elements are provision of adequate equipment and technical capabilities for field and laboratory settings and standardization of protocols ($60 million per year).

- Establishing regional institutions to provide interdisciplinary research integrating human sciences and natural sciences and bringing together managers from government, academia, and the private sector ($60 million per year).

- Initiating an integrated National Science Foundation program to promote effective multidisciplinary research on a scale commensurate with contemporary issues in limnology ($10 million per year).

Anticipated immediate benefits from enhanced institutional support for freshwater science include strengthened research, education, and technology needed to respond effectively to critical issues, assurance that issues are evaluated at scales commensurate with the scientific and social problems, and development of multidisciplinary approaches to increasingly complex problems. Anticipated benefits to the nation include increased health and safety of U.S. citizens, less waste and more efficient use of the nation's resources, greater responsiveness of management to societal needs, a greater ability to respond to future threats, and increased environmental security.

The physical and intellectual infrastructure for the FWI can be enhanced through the following:

- Establishing a freshwater biodiversity center to provide systematic and comprehensive data on freshwater biodiversity, to develop sensitive biotic indices on environmental change, and to enhance predictability and accuracy in monitoring programs ($15 million per year).

- Establishing an array of long-term and altered research sites with specific freshwater emphases ($20 million per year).

- Strengthening education and communication to provide innovative and broad-based training above and beyond traditional efforts for students and professionals in the freshwater disciplines. This includes support for continuing education and "retooling" for midcareer scientists and managers, workshops on newly evolving technologies and concepts, and cooperative public and private sector training grants ($15 million per year).

Anticipated benefits to the nation from an enhanced physical and intellectual infrastructure include systematic and comprehensive data and innovative approaches to biodiversity issues, an ability to address linkages between human and environmental sustainability, and a continued high level of literacy about freshwater ecosystems and their management.

Freshwater ecosystems play a central role in our nation's social, economic, environmental, and political mosaic. Freshwater scientists and managers are increasingly called upon to respond to disruptions of water and freshwater resources that threaten the quality of human life, the environmental sustainability of the biosphere, and the viability of human cultures. Unfortunately, fundamental deficiencies exist in our national infrastructure supporting freshwater sciences and management. A primary goal of the FWI research agenda is to assist in the development of a national strategy to address these deficiencies, and to help ensure that water resource managers and policy makers have adequate and timely information to protect, utilize, and enhance water resources. The research agenda and its implementation, recommended by the nation's freshwater scientific community, identifies high-priority research areas and proposes a conceptual framework for building a durable infrastructure that will position the United States for the issues of the next century. While improvements will be made as the FWI evolves, it is urgent that a comprehensive, integrated freshwater program be implemented if the nation is to eventually resolve water-related issues in a realistic manner.

1

Fresh Water and the Freshwater Imperative

Importance of Fresh Water to Society

Human society depends on fresh water and the resources associated with it. Freshwater systems provide water for drinking, hydropower, irrigation, cooling, and cleaning; products such as food, plants, and minerals; and services such as recreation, waste purification, transportation, and aesthetics. Nationally and globally there is abundant evidence that freshwater resources are being rapidly depleted and their quality severely degraded. Depletion results directly from consumption as well as from the effects of human actions, direct and indirect, on the environment. Degradation—unfavorable change in distribution, abundance, and quality of water and aquatic ecosystems—represents a threat to the quality of human life, perhaps even to the sustainability of the biosphere and the long-term vitality of human society.*

Human societies often naively operate as if they have an unlimited capability to alter water resources and the landscape without degrading the ability of those resources to meet human needs. Moreover, societies often act on the erroneous assumption that increasingly complex technology can continue to replace lost ecological values. The rate of degradation of freshwater resources worldwide is alarming (see chapter 2), a reflection of both the acceleration of human-caused environmental change and the sensitivity of freshwater ecosystems to change. Collectively, lakes, rivers, and wetlands integrate all the human and natural activities and events occurring in a watershed. Rivers act as "the arteries of the continents," and lakes and wetlands act as integrative sensors of air pollution, climate

*In this book, *sustainability* is used in the sense proposed by the World Commission on Environment and Development [1987]: "the ability to meet the needs of the present generation without compromising the ability of future generations to meet their needs." Also, please note terms such as *limnology, freshwater ecology, inland water ecology,* and *aquatic ecology* are used interchangeably; although subtle differences between the terms are recognized, all are equally descriptive of the breadth of freshwater sciences.

change, and land use change (Degens, Kempe, and Richey 1991). The characteristics of waters, like the characteristics of blood, are diagnostic of the integrity or health of watersheds (Sioli 1975). In addition to being diagnostic, the attributes of fresh waters determine the ultimate success of human and other life.

Of the many uses of fresh water, potable water is perhaps the most crucial resource for the maintenance of human societies. Yet fresh water is limited in total supply, unevenly distributed, and often of unacceptable quality, particularly in areas where supply is limited. Both the quantity and quality of water are shaped by virtually all components of a watershed and by biological and physical processes inherently characteristic of the groundwater, lakes, ponds, rivers, streams, and wetlands within which the water resides.

A complete understanding of the multiple factors influencing water quality and aquatic habitats requires a broad, multidisciplinary approach. Consideration of water as a commodity or resource in isolation from its associated chemical, physical, and biological properties has led to disastrous consequences for managers (National Research Council 1987; Stanford and Ward 1992a; Lee 1993; Oremland 1994). Application of basic principles of aquatic ecology is essential in any comprehensive research plan for the nation's or world's fresh water (Karr 1991; Likens 1992).

Addressing Freshwater Issues

Addressing problems of water resource degradation requires an expanded understanding and evaluation of the nature of freshwater problems. It requires identification and development of appropriate societal responses to mitigate damage to natural resources (figure 1.1), including development and evaluation of restoration techniques. Effective approaches to accomplish these tasks depend on partnerships at several levels: among natural scientists in complementary disciplines, among natural and social scientists, and among scientists, policy makers, and natural resource managers. Partnerships among natural scientists include those spanning traditional physical, chemical, and biological disciplines and addressing the full range of interacting environments, such as groundwaters, lakes, streams, and wetlands and land, oceans, air, and ice. This breadth is encompassed within the science of limnology, or freshwater ecology, the study of inland waters in all their aspects.

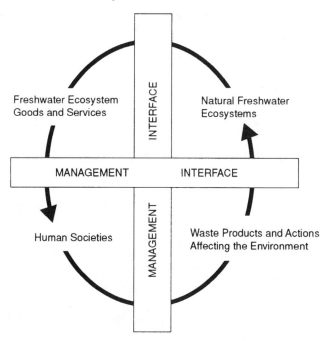

Figure 1.1 Interaction of human societies and Natural Freshwater Ecosystems. Ecosystems produce goods and services that are used by society—often at minimal cost—and human activities and waste products may have profound effects on freshwater ecosystems. The management interface is not always effective at ensuring that feedbacks between parts of this system are beneficial.

Partnerships among natural and social scientists are necessary to produce not only high-quality science but also science in its most usable form. Unfortunately, these partnerships have not yet developed into an identifiable transdisciplinary science. However, interactive partnerships among freshwater scientists, policy makers, and resource managers are essential for developing a comprehensive approach to integrating freshwater sciences with management of freshwater systems. Early and continued interaction of scientists, managers, and policy makers will produce useful results that can, through adaptive management and bounded conflict (in the sense of Lee 1993), lead to improved management systems for fresh waters.

Two key challenges faced by freshwater scientists are distinguishing natural from human-induced changes and effectively assessing cumulative effects. These require long-term studies appropriate to the

Multidisciplinary Teams in Limnology

Multidisciplinary scientific teams at the Experimental Lakes Area (ELA) in Ontario, Canada, and at Lake Mendota, Wisconsin, have been extraordinarily successful in solving major environmental problems, despite the usual difficulties in understanding complex limnological systems. These North American sites provide models for additional U.S. initiatives. Ecosystem-scale experiments by integrated teams of hydrologists, biologists, geochemists, and soil scientists at the ELA are providing the predictive understanding of natural ecosystems necessary to identify and solve such problems as cultural eutrophication, acidification, and heavy metal pollution. For example, the ELA team has elucidated the effects of specific nutrients on water quality and clarity, providing new insights into the roles of phosphorus and nitrogen, rather than inorganic carbon, in limiting primary productivity in nutrient-poor ecosystems (Schindler 1977). The Wisconsin team manipulated the food web of Lake Mendota to demonstrate how addition of top predators to the lake increased water clarity through the cascading effects of predation (Kitchell 1992), showing that the clarity of eutrophic lakes is controlled by both nutrient inputs and intensity of predation on herbivorous prey.

Other insights from the ELA and Wisconsin studies show that effects of acidity are first seen as changes in species composition of lakes and that microorganisms generating alkalinity in sediments can play a critical role in ameliorating the effects of acid rain on lakes (Schindler et al. 1985). Working with physical and chemical oceanographers, the ELA limnologists unraveled the complex mechanics of gas exchange across the air-water interface, an achievement that was instrumental in understanding these vital processes in the ocean, a major component of the planet's biogeochemical carbon cycle. These examples underscore an urgent need for a national effort to organize and support teams of

temporal and spatial scales of factors controlling aquatic systems and framing water resource issues. Increasing evidence, for example, suggests that changes in global climate can alter or decrease water resources in complex and poorly predicted ways (Smith 1991; Carpenter et al. 1992; Melack 1992). As freshwater issues become more complex, researchers need to develop the capacity to make predictions on temporal scales of 10 to 100 years and at spatial scales that include air-land-water interactions at the watershed scale (approximately 100 square kilometers) or larger. At broad spatiotemporal scales, interacting effects of numerous agents of change are superimposed. Habitat destruction, deforestation, acid precipitation, eutrophication, toxic pollution, climate change, overfishing, and introduction of exotic species act simultaneously and cumulatively and as such may have effects that exceed those of any single agent of change.

Currently, the issues surrounding fresh waters on a national scale are

scientists from diverse disciplines to address problems involving human-accelerated environmental change in aquatic ecosystems.

This lake in northwestern Ontario, Canada, demostrates the vital role of phosphorus in eutrophication. The far basin, fertilized with phosphorus, nitrogen, and carbon, was covered by an algal bloom within two months. However, no increase in algae or change in species composition was observed in the near basin, which received similar quantities of nitrogen and carbon but no phosphorus (Schindler 1974). (Photo copyright 1974 by the AAAS.)

more extensive and complex than any one agency or institution can address effectively (Turner et al. 1990; Lee 1993). Unfortunately, long-term watershed-scale or regional-scale studies are not the norm for freshwater sciences. Yet this is the appropriate scale for integration of social, environmental, and economic issues influencing watershed characteristics. It is a scale toward which limnologists and resource managers need to direct more energy and expertise (Naiman 1992).

Because of the massive changes taking place in our aquatic systems and water supplies, only a short time remains for developing a predictive understanding of freshwater ecosystems and their management. Society and its leaders need to work expeditiously to set a positive agenda. To delay threatens the sustainability of the environment and hence the stability of human society. As Kai Lee (1993) warns: "One of the peculiar commonplaces of our time is the realization that civilized life cannot continue in its present form."

Objective of the Freshwater Imperative Research Agenda

The objective of the Freshwater Imperative (FWI) research agenda is to identify research opportunities and frontiers for inland water ecology (limnology) for the 1990s and beyond. This book is a comprehensive integration of ideas and concerns from recent workshops and symposia on research directions for lake, stream, and wetland science (for example, see Lehman 1986; Carpenter 1988; Stanford and Covich 1988; National Research Council 1991; Firth and Fisher 1992; Naiman 1992). The process of developing the FWI research agenda provided a broad-based opportunity for natural scientists to evaluate the state of knowledge in various disciplines, identify fundamental gaps in knowledge within and among disciplines, suggest program guidelines, identify future research and educational activities, and make specific suggestions for implementation. This book is intended to assist government agencies and private institutions in establishing long-term program directions for freshwater research that relate directly to improved regional watershed-level management and human sustainability.

The FWI research agenda addresses a strategic, long-term goal: to ensure that water resource managers and policy makers have adequate and timely scientific information to protect, utilize, and enhance the nation's water resources. This book can contribute significantly to the development of a national strategy for freshwater science that includes research, applications and technology transfer, and education and outreach. Such a freshwater science strategy requires an ever-improving infrastructure responsive to the evolving knowledge that eventually can provide a predictive understanding of freshwater resources and ecosystems.

2

Status of Fresh Waters and Challenges Ahead

Degradation of Freshwater Resources

In the United States and other countries, degradation of water resources results in (1) biological impoverishment, (2) altered hydrologic regimes, and (3) risks to human health and quality of life. These three issues highlight the critical need for a freshwater research strategy that defines specific priority areas (figure 2.1). The strategic goal of the Freshwater Imperative is directly related to these issues, as is our opportunity as a nation to develop an ever-improving understanding and management of freshwaters (see chapters 3 and 4). The Freshwater Imperative is especially crucial at this time as the nation faces an unprecedented decline in the quantity and quality of its freshwater systems.

Biological Impoverishment

Biological impoverishment is the antithesis of ecological integrity—maintenance of the physical, chemical, and biological systems necessary for sustaining an acceptable quality of life. Declines in the integrity or health of biological support systems on earth are an ominous signal to human society (Karr 1993). Two major elements constitute ecological systems: the components, as measured by the numbers or types of plants, animals, chemicals, or biomass, and the processes, as measured by the rates of exchange of materials and energy among the components. This concept of biological impoverishment is roughly reflective of biological diversity but is a broader measure than genetic or species diversity.

Biological impoverishment results from human failure to recognize that we depend on the integrity of earth's life support processes. These biological processes include predation, photosynthesis, gas fluxes, and nutrient availability, as well as a host of other processes related to nutrient

The United States Water Problem

About 25% of the water that falls on the United States each year as precipitation infiltrates the soil and recharges local aquifers. In 1985 about 22% of the freshwater withdrawals in the United States were from ground water (Moody 1990). These withdrawals provided drinking water for about 53% of the U.S. population. Eight of the 50 states (Arizona, Arkansas, California, Florida, Idaho, Kansas, Nebraska, Texas) use 66% of the total ground water withdrawn each year in the U.S., and most of this water is used for irrigation (Moody 1990).

Every day the public water systems of the United States provide, on average, about 160 gallons (605 liters) of water per person. Considering the total population (250,000,000) in the United States, this requires about 40 billion gallons (1.5×1011 liters) of water a day. Based on the expected population increase for the United States, in 50 years some 50 billion gallons (1.9×1011 liters) of water per day will be required if the per capita use stays the same. On average it requires about 100,000 gallons (378,500 liters) of water to produce one automobile, 60,000 gallons (227,100 liters) to produce one ton of steel, 1,500 gallons (5,678 liters) to produce one cotton dress, and 10 gallons (38 liters) to produce one copy of a book like this one (Powledge 1984). A typical family of four in the United States uses about 10 gallons (38 liters) per day for drinking and cooking, about 15 gallons (57 liters) per day to wash dishes, 98 gallons (371 liters) per day for toilets, 80 gallons (303 liters) per day for bathing, 35 gallons (132 liters) per day for laundry and about 100 gallons (379 liters) per day for watering the lawn, washing the car and so forth. Thus, about 338 gallons (1279 liters) per day are used by a typical family of four, of which only 3% is used for cooking and drinking. Typically, a toilet in the U.S. requires about 4 gallons (15 liters) for each flush. The so-called water-saver models require about 2.5 gallons (9.5 liters). Such unnecessary waste of water in the U.S. is far greater than in most other countries of the world where per capita uses are often less than 5 gallons (19 liters) per day.

cycling, genetics, and reproduction. In addition, physical processes affect the rate of biological processes—for example, water circulation affects algal photosynthesis rates, nutrient supply, and dilution of pollutants. The interactions between biological and physical processes are integral to maintenance of ecosystem integrity.

Biological impoverishment takes several forms: habitat destruction and fragmentation, release of toxic organic materials and excess nutrients, acid deposition, spread of exotic species, noxious algal growth, overharvesting of fish and wildlife, and altered thermal regimes, among others (table 2.1).

Habitat Destruction and Fragmentation Elimination or irreversible alteration of aquatic habitats is ubiquitous because human populations and

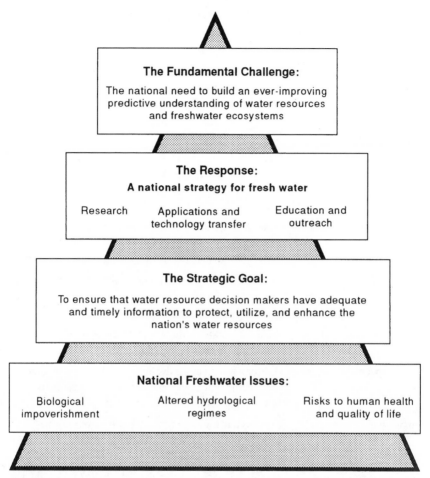

The Fundamental Challenge:

The national need to build an ever-improving predictive understanding of water resources and freshwater ecosystems

The Response:

A national strategy for fresh water

Research   Applications and   Education and
                technology transfer   outreach

The Strategic Goal:

To ensure that water resource decision makers have adequate and timely information to protect, utilize, and enhance the nation's water resources

National Freshwater Issues:

Biological   Altered hydrological   Risks to human health
impoverishment   regimes   and quality of life

Figure 2.1   Elements of a Freshwater Research Strategy for Meeting Critical National Needs

activities center on water, and water is treated as a sump for human activities (Turner et al. 1990; Moyle and Leidy 1992; Dynesius and Nilsson 1994). As a result, the cumulative effects of habitat destruction are considerable. Habitat destruction may be direct and obvious, such as channelization of streams or riprapping of lake shores, or a secondary result of other actions, such as downstream effects of dam construction or sediment and nutrient runoff from altered land use). Already wetlands in the United States have declined by 40–60 percent (Dahl 1990), while riparian forests have been destroyed on about 70 percent of the rivers of the coterminous United States (Swift 1984). The Nationwide Rivers Inventory estimated a total of 5,200,000 kilometers (3,230,000 miles) of streams in the

Table 2.1   Factors Contributing to Biological
Impoverishment of Aquatic Ecosystems

Component	Explanation
Habitat destruction and fragmentation	Aquatic habitats are increasingly being eliminated or irreversibly altered by human populations and activities centered on streams, lakes, wetlands, and estuaries and by use of aquatic systems as sumps for land-based human activities
Toxic organic materials	The introduction of a wide array of organic compounds, many of which are xenobiotic, into aquatic environments is significant and in many cases continues unabated
Nitrogen contamination	At high concentrations nitrogen is toxic to humans, particularly young children, and in many areas it is a major contributor to acid deposition (as nitric acid)
Toxic metals	Dynamics of metals are controlled by the unique physical and chemical environment as well as by biotic accumulations within the food web
Acid deposition	Acid deposition continues unabated in spite of the 1990 amendments to the Clean Air Act
Exotic species	A strong influence on declining biodiversity and faunal homogenization is the spread of exotic organisms through deliberate and accidental introductions
Toxic algal blooms	Freshwaters are experiencing, with increasing frequency, nuisance algal and cyanobacteria blooms, some of which are toxic to the aquatic biota and humans
Harvest of aquatic resources	Harvesting of freshwater fish and shellfish for food and other products has declined precipitously in recent decades due to habitat destruction and overharvesting
Altered thermal regimes	Interaction of science and management remains poor with respect to thermal effects and their impacts

contiguous forty-eight states, but only 2 percent (less than 10,000 kilometers) have sufficiently high-quality features to be worthy of federal protection as relatively pristine rivers (Benke 1990). In North America north of Mexico, in Europe, and in the republics of the former Soviet Union, seventy-seven percent of the total water discharge of the 139 largest river systems is strongly or moderately affected by fragmentation of the river channels by dams and by water regulation resulting from reservoir operation, interbasin diversion, and irrigation (Dynesius and Nilsson 1994). These conditions indicate that many types of river systems have been lost and that populations of many riverine species have become highly fragmented. Destruction of specific aquatic and riparian habitats also causes fragmentation among remaining habitats, which significantly influences the movement of water, materials, and organisms across the landscape. In addition, many organisms require several types of habitat to support different life history stages. Selective destruction of some habitats within a drainage network reduces the viability of populations in subtle ways that have severe long-term consequences for particular species. Destruction and fragmentation of habitats increase the costs of cleanup and decimate resources of considerable value to society, such as salmon (*Oncorhynchus* sp.) in the Pacific Northwest. A predictive knowledge of how habitat destruction and fragmentation affect aquatic resources can permit judicious planning that avoids the need for expensive restoration efforts.

Although the extent of destruction, fragmentation, and defragmentation of aquatic habitats is widely recognized, many fundamental questions remain:

- At what level of alteration do habitat destruction and fragmentation become irreversible, especially when viewed at different spatial and temporal scales?

- What is the extent to which degraded systems can be restored, especially when the definition of "natural" is likely to vary or to change over time as cultural values and perceptions change?

- What are the characteristics of a regional strategy for protection of aquatic biodiversity and environmental integrity in the face of continuous habitat degradation?

- What are the needs of society, and what are the costs and benefits of alternatives that address those needs?

Exotic Species A major cause of biological impoverishment is the spread of exotic aquatic and riparian organisms through both deliberate and accidental introductions. The results are loss of biodiversity as well as faunal homogenization. For example, the zebra mussel (*Dreissena polymorpha*), Asiatic clam (*Corbicula fluminea*), and other molluscs; purple loosestrife (*Lythrum salicarium*), eurasian watermilfoil (*Myriophyllum spicatum*), and other macrophytes; carp (*Cyprinus carpio*), grass carp (*Ctenopharyngodon idella*), rainbow smelt (*Osmerus mordax*), sea lamprey (*Petromyzon marinus*), and other fishes; and other organisms that have been introduced into the nation's waters represent major threats to the health of freshwater ecosystems.

Invasion of freshwater ecosystems by exotic organisms has detrimental and irreversible consequences. Exotic organisms compete with native species for light, water, and other resources and frequently displace and cause extirpation or extinction of native species. Exotic species also interfere with natural successional processes, harm domestic animals, alter natural disturbance regimes, and even alter the dynamics of freshwater ecosystems by affecting geochemical and geophysical conditions and processes. A predictive understanding of their effects and the processes by which they affect native flora and fauna will require addressing the following questions:

- What ecological conditions allow these species to become established?

- What allows buildup of populations to nuisance levels and then, often, a subsequent decline to lower levels?

- How do resource managers decide when to count on a population crash to avoid expensive and unnecessary control efforts?

- Are some habitats especially prone to invasion? Is this feature related to earlier human disturbance? How will global climate change influence invasions and extinctions?

- What are the natural means of dispersal and the natural rates of invasion and extinction of aquatic systems that differ in degree of isolation and that often may be "islandlike"?

- What are the effects of diseases and parasites carried by introduced species?

In general, the role of disease in ecological systems has not been studied adequately, and the dynamics and long-term influence of disease outbreaks are simply not known.

Overharvesting of Fishery and Wildlife Resources   Harvests of fish and shellfish for food and other industries (for example, use of mollusc shells in manufacture of buttons) have declined precipitously in recent decades. Although much of the decline may be attributed to the influence of other human actions described in this book, overharvesting for sport and commercial purposes often is a factor. Consistent patterns of overharvesting are due to four common scientific and social characteristics (Ludwig, Hilborn, and Waters 1993): (1) Wealth or the prospect of wealth generates political and social power that is used to promote exploitation. (2) Scientific understanding and consensus are hampered by a lack of proper controls and replicates; thus, each new problem involves learning about a new system. (3) The complexity of the underlying biological and physical systems precludes a reductionist approach to management; therefore, optimum levels of harvest must be determined by trial and error. And (4) large levels of natural variability mask the effects of overexploitation. Initial overexploitation is not detectable until it is severe and often irreversible. Further misguided and ecologically uninformed efforts to overcome population declines may exacerbate the problem, as with release of hatchery fish (Hilborn 1992; Meffe 1992). In addition, models fundamental to fisheries management, such as the stock recruitment model, have proven inadequate (Hall 1988), seriously affecting the ability of resource managers to provide for long-term productivity of species-specific fisheries. Any comprehensive approach to treating biological impoverishment requires information on population dynamics, harvest design, and implementation that provides a sustainable resource for the long term. Questions to be addressed include the following:

- What is needed to produce realistic, useful models and innovative ecosystem management strategies that can reduce uncertainties about population characteristics?

- What are the long-term effects of single-species management on ecosystem-level characteristics? How do focused management strategies reverberate through an entire ecosystem?

- Considering the inherent variability and connectivity of ecological systems, is it realistic to expect aquatic resource management to be a precise science?

Altered Thermal Regimes   Environmental changes that alter heat budgets and distribution of temperature in aquatic systems are well known, and much has been done to alleviate the problem in some cases. However, the complexity of the problem and the nature and pathways of thermal influences on the integrity of freshwater ecosystems remain key issues in affecting biological impoverishment. Density differences and complicated mixing regimes of water from different sources create complex management problems. Furthermore, thermal alterations in streams resulting from destruction of riparian forests have important local and downstream effects, as does discharge from certain types of reservoirs. Interaction of science and management with respect to thermal effects and their consequences is still in its infancy. For example, it is known that even small changes in the temperature regime of a water body (approximately 1°C) can have significant effects on its biota (Ward and Stanford 1982). Given the potential for major temperature alterations associated with global climate change, surface waters will probably undergo widespread temperature changes, with concomitant effects on physical, chemical, and biological processes as well as on human use and adaptation to climate change (Smith 1991; Firth and Fisher 1992; Karieva, Kingsolver and Huey 1993). Two areas merit further study:

• How will subtle alterations to aquatic temperature regimes affect community composition, reproductive success, and the spread of exotic species and disease?

• Can temperature regimes be managed so as to control community composition, productivity, and water quality?

Toxic Organic Compounds   Introduction of a wide array of organic compounds, many of which are xenobiotic, into aquatic environments is significant at local and regional scales and in many cases has continued unabated for decades. The eloquent description of the dramatic biological effect of organic contamination by DDT in Rachel Carson's *Silent Spring* (1962) became the foundation of the environmental movement. In 1979, Aldicarb was discovered in 96 wells on Long Island, and 1,2-dibromo-3-chloropropane (DBCP) was found in more than 2,000 wells in California (Goodrich, Lykins, and Clark 1991). Historically, concern about the influence of this class of contaminants centered on acute toxicity. We now recognize that toxic organic compounds have chronic effects, especially as inducers of immunologic and reproductive dysfunction and as hormone inhibitors (Colborn and Clement 1992). Recent demonstration of their effects as hormone inhibitors and intergenerational consequences of the use of toxic organics is especially alarming (Colborn et al. 1990; Colborn and Clement 1992). Ecological effects of toxic substances are commonly found at concentrations much lower than those required for acute toxicity in laboratory studies (Schindler 1987; Howarth 1991). Such effects often include disruption of food webs, interference with reproduction, and reduced growth and survival of young stages of aquatic organisms. This contaminant effect remains a dominant threat to both components and processes in biological systems.

No integrated understanding of the effects of toxic organic contaminants exists. Top predators in many regional ecosystems, such as salmon (*Oncorhynchus* sp.), the great blue heron (*Ardea herodias*), and Lake

Ontario herring gulls (*Larus argentatus*), seem especially at risk of extirpation through reproductive dysfunction (Colborn and Clement 1992). Even our current rudimentary understanding of the pathways of toxic organic compounds at individual and ecological levels suggests that the approaches of conventional risk assessment are flawed because they do not deal with the commonly ignored dimension of uncertainty (Clark 1991). Uncertainty derives from lack of knowledge of the detailed dynamics of an environmental risk or lack of recognition that a risk exists. The urgency of addressing toxic organic compounds is increased by the growing realization that many organic chemicals are much more long-lived in the environment than once thought. For example, atrazine, a widely used herbicide, is now widespread in groundwater in the midwestern United States. In Lake Ontario, it is believed to persist for as long as a decade (Schottler and Eisenreich 1994). The following questions are in urgent need of investigation:

- Is it possible to predict the persistence and ecological activity of toxic organic compounds from their molecular structure and the characteristics of the environment?

- Can possible synergistic relations between toxic organic compounds and other molecules in the environment be predicted theoretically?

Toxic Metals There is considerable knowledge about the chemistry of toxic metals in freshwater systems, biological uptake of metals, and concentrations of metals in biotic tissues. However, little is known about the ecological interactions of toxic metals in aquatic environments. Sources of metals include atmospheric deposition, runoff from modified watersheds, and mining and industrial activities. Storm water runoff is a major source of metal pollution in urban surface waters. The Environmental Protection Agency's Nationwide Urban Runoff study found that the most common pollutants in urban runoff were heavy metals such as copper, lead, and zinc. In many cases, discharge concentrations exceeded both ambient water quality criteria and drinking water standards of the EPA. All thirteen metals on the EPA's priority pollutant list were detected in urban runoff samples, all but three at frequencies of detection that exceeded 10 percent (Environmental Protection Agency 1983). The dynamics of metals are controlled by the physical and chemical environment of a specific water body (pH and alkalinity, presence of anaerobic conditions, and organic enrichment) as well as by the incorporation, movement, and biomagnification of metals in a food web (Lindberg, Stokes, and Goldberg 1987; Bloom, Waters, and Hurley 1991; Watras et al. 1991).

Mercury Contamination of Freshwater Resources

The discovery of high levels of mercury and other toxic metals in lakes remote from industrial activity points out the need to understand linkages between human activities and natural resources via unsuspected pathways (Porcella 1994). Concentrations of mercury in fish high enough to raise serious concerns about human health have recently been reported in widespread areas of the United States, Canada, and Scandinavia, a major environmental problem that was forcefully brought to the public's attention on the front page of *USA Today* and in *Time* and *Newsweek* magazines.

Large fish usually contain greater amounts of mercury than do small fish because of biomagnification through food webs. Obviously, this fact is of direct concern to both harvester and consumers of fish. Transport of mercury from industrial sites to remote areas is suspected to occur primarily through the atmosphere. There also seems to be a connection with acid rain, as fish from acidified lakes normally contain more mercury in their tissues than do fish from nonacid lakes. It appears that mercury pollution of lakes has the potential to emerge as one of the major environmental problems of the early twenty-first century.

Important examples of metal contaminants are mercury, cadmium, and copper. Because of its toxicity, mercury pollution may become a major environmental problem in the 1990s. Much attention has focused on the relationship between surface impoundments and methyl mercury concentrations. It has been demonstrated that mercury methylation is enhanced by increased availability of organic carbon and that increased decomposition of organic matter is a major cause of increased methylation in newly flooded reservoirs. A study of natural lakes in Canada found a rapid threefold increase in mercury levels in northern pike (*Esoxlucius*) and walleye (*Stizostedion vitreum*) following impoundment (from levels of $0.2-0.3$ µg/g to $0.5-1.0$ µg/g) (Bodaly, Hecky, and Fudge 1984; Nash 1993).

The current lack of knowledge about the basic biogeochemistry of aquatic systems confounds the problem of dealing with metal contamination. Particularly poorly understood are the roles of atmospheric delivery and remobilization of toxic metals in fresh waters and the movement of metals through the terrestrial portion of the watershed to the water. The following questions remain:

- How is cycling of toxic metals linked to the biogeochemical cycles of other elements?

- What mechanisms are available in the ecological system either to sequester metals for long time periods or to detoxify them?

- How do toxic metals, singly and in various combinations, affect the population dynamics of a water body's biota?

Nitrogen Contamination Another form of water contamination, although not usually as toxic as contamination by organic chemicals or metals, is that caused by excess nitrogen in fresh water. Nitrogen contamination affects both surface water and groundwater supplies. Sources of nitrogen contamination range from the atmosphere (originating from industrial and transportation sources) to sewage, agricultural runoff, deforestation, direct inputs from industrial activities, and other watershed disturbances. At high concentrations, nitrogen can be toxic to humans, particularly young children. For example, methemoglobinemia is caused by nitrites, which result from conversion of nitrates in the low-acidity stomachs of infants. This so-called blue baby syndrome occurs when the oxygen-carrying capacity of hemoglobin is blocked, causing suffocation (Harte et al., 1991; Nash 1993). Nitrogen as nitric acid is the major form of acid deposition in many areas. Widespread evidence suggests that nitrogen contamination is growing in severity throughout most of the United States (Turner and Rabalais 1991; Cole et al. 1993). For example, a 1987 study found that in 5 percent of the sampled counties, more than 25 percent of the wells sampled had nitrate concentrations that exceeded federal drinking water criteria of 10 mg/L NO_3-N (Nielsen and Lee 1987).

Nitrogen also stimulates plant production and can cause eutrophication in water bodies, including many streams, rivers, and lakes and the majority of estuaries and coastal seas. The problem of eutrophication in estuaries is particularly acute and growing, with increasing incidence of anoxic waters and toxic algal blooms (National Research Council 1992). Much of the nitrogen delivered to coastal waters comes from the terrestrial drainage network; basic research on the biogeochemistry and microbial transformation of nitrogen in fresh waters is essential to resolving the problem. For example, it is known that wetlands and riparian forests are important in processing nitrogen (Pinay et al. 1990; Johnson 1991a). The following areas require further study:

- To what degree can wetlands and riparian forests absorb nitrogen before becoming saturated and leaking it into groundwater and streams?

- What are the fundamental characteristics of wetlands and riparian forests that allow them to be effective filters for nitrogen and other potentially harmful nutrients?

Toxic Algal Blooms With increasing frequency, many freshwater bodies and coastal marine waters are experiencing nuisance algae (or cyanobacteria) and macrophyte growths, some of which have toxic effects on the aquatic biota and humans. The causes of these blooms are not well understood, but they appear to result from changes in the balance of water supply, temperature, and nutrients (Anderson, Galloway, and Joseph 1992). Because of the capacity of nuisance organisms for exponential growth, their populations build rapidly and episodically and without warning. Proper management requires an ability to forecast toxic algal blooms. Efforts to resolve this problem require innovative research agendas that draw from principles of algal and macrophyte physiology (photosynthetic and nutrient physiology), physical limnology, and biogeochemistry. In many circumstances, factors initiating blooms in coastal waters have both freshwater and estuarine elements. Questions include the following:

- How do nutrient and water runoff from the watershed interact with estuarine ecosystems to initiate algal blooms?

- What ecological factors control the severity and longevity of algal blooms?

Unfortunately, conventional institutional boundaries between freshwater and marine research continue to impede progress on these fundamental research questions.

Acid Deposition   Despite the considerable expenditures of the National Acid Precipitation Assessment Program (NAPAP) during the 1980s, the complex influences of acidity on biological systems and their long-term interaction with regional geochemistry still are not understood at a level that allows resolution of the problem or prediction of long-term effects on freshwater ecosystems and human society. Although the program succeded in reducing uncertainty about the spatial extent and direct effects of acid deposition, it severely underfunded research designed to assess the effects on biological and geochemical processes and their interactions in diverse freshwater (and terrestrial) systems (Likens 1992). Acid rain deposition continues unabated in spite of the 1990 amendments to the Clean Air Act and is likely to remain unabated through the end of the twentieth century. Lack of adequate predictive knowledge and lack of ongoing research on and monitoring of the ecological effects of sulfur and nitrogen in the face of continuing sulfur and nitrogen emissions are serious deficiencies. Despite efforts to reduce acid-causing atmospheric emissions, acid rain is still a major cause of ecosystem degradation (Likens 1992).The following questions need to be addressed:

- What are the important interactions between acid deposition and other environmental stresses, both natural and human induced, on freshwater ecosystems?

- Is it possible to predict the relative roles of sulfur and nitrogen in the biogeochemical and ecological changes accompanying restoration of water after acidification?

Altered Hydrologic Regimes

Human actions have altered the hydrology of watersheds and freshwater systems in numerous ways, with direct and indirect consequences to the maintenance of human societies (Magnuson 1978; Petts 1984; Lvovich and White 1990). Engineering structures increase or decrease hydrologic connectivity of freshwater systems, rates of water movement, and transport and movement of organisms, materials, and heat. The totality of these human-induced alterations has affected water resources in nearly every sector of the United States (and the earth). Yet we have dangerously little understanding of the long-term and widespread consequences of these actions (Dynesius and Nilsson 1994).

Agriculture, forestry, urbanization, industrialization, channelization, and construction of transportation corridors alter the terrestrial and aquatic components of watersheds. These in turn alter water absorption, infiltration, runoff, and erodibility. Hence, changes take place in the flow (volume and timing) of water, sediments, nutrients, and organisms in river channels, lake basins, wetlands, and groundwaters (table 2.2). Altered land use also reduces the water storage capacity of floodplains and increases the likelihood of severe floods. An understanding of the dynamics of "healthy" watersheds is urgently needed to provide models essential for interpreting patterns observed in modified watersheds and for effectively restorating ecological systems throughout the United States (Naiman 1992).

Altered Stream and River Flow Construction of dams and diversions and modification of watersheds have greatly altered the natural flow regime in streams and rivers (Petts 1984; Calow and Petts 1992; Reisner 1993; Dynesius and Nilsson 1994). Some streams are dewatered, while the water flow of others is increased. Existing flow regimes, particularly in large rivers and western drainages, largely reflect human demands for water rather than natural cycles. In addition, hydraulic properties such as mixing, turbulence, stream power, and shear stress have been modified,

Table 2.2   Effects of Altered Hydrologic Regimes on Freshwater Ecosystems

Alteration	Explanation
Watershed characteristics	Agriculture, forestry, urbanization, industrialization, and channelization influence water absorption, infiltration, erodibility, and runoff
Stream and river flow	Construction of dams and diversions and alteration of watersheds have greatly influenced natural flow regimes and the dynamics of organisms adapted to those regimes
Lakes and wetlands	Direct management activities and indirect human activities have changed lake and wetland water levels and their natural thermal regimes
Groundwater and surface water-groundwater interactions	Groundwater is overexploited, aquifers are being depleted, salt water is intruding, and subsurface organisms are becoming endangered
Desertification and salinization	Regulation and active movement of waters as well as a changing global climate regime have resulted in locally severe desertification and intrusion of salt water into formerly freshwater aquifers

with substantial effects on biological communities and physicochemical processes. As a result, wetlands and riparian forests have been lost (Swift 1984; Karr 1991), native fishes and invertebrates have become rare or endangered (Minckley and Deacon 1991; Stanford 1993; Bogan 1995), and major commercial fisheries have been decimated (for example, Columbia River salmon). Although some specific aspects of altered streams have been intensely studied, especially in regard to instream flow requirements of fish, much remains to be learned about how altered flow regimes affect overall biodiversity and biotic interactions in stream ecosystems and how such streams can be managed to minimize conflicts between environmental and human needs for flowing water. For example:

- What are the effects of changing shear stress on benthic community composition and productivity?

- What are the physical characteristics of flowing water that maintain ecosystem integrity rather than single species?

Altered Lake and Wetland Hydrology   Lakes varying in size from local wetlands and ponds to the Great Lakes have altered water levels and mixing patterns because of direct, active management of water supplies,

Influence of Wetlands on Water Quality

Biotic and abiotic processes in wetlands interact in ways that can be beneficial to downstream water quality. Mechanisms include sedimentation (and associated phosphorus retention), sorption, vegetative nutrient uptake, and microbial transformation of nutrients and toxins (Wetzel 1983). The pollutant-processing capabilities of wetlands have led to widespread use of natural wetlands for waste disposal (sewage effluent, storm water runoff). Unfortunately, such projects often have been initiated with inadequate understanding of wetland-pollutant dynamics and capacities, and short-term successes have led to longer-term failures, such as complete alteration of wetland communities and their conversion from pollutant sinks to pollutant sources (Johnston 1991a). Thus, active use of wetlands for pollutant amelioration requires a balance between sustaining downstream water quality and sustaining wetland health.

Artificial wetlands have been constructed to mimic natural pollutant control properties (Hammer 1989; Johnston 1993). Although their use removes the risk to natural wetlands, many unknowns remain about how artificial wetlands function. There is also a need to verify that using wetlands for pollution disposal does not merely convert surface water pollution into groundwater pollution via leakage.

Natural wetlands' ability to improve or degrade water quality is highly dependent on their patterns of water input and output, and thier distribution. At the watershed scale, the location of wetlands relative to streams (Johnston, Detenbeck, and Niemi 1990) and lakes (Johnston et al. 1984; Detenbeck, Johnston, and Niemi 1993) greatly influences their individual and collective capacity to improve water quality. A wetland may have high pollutant reduction potential, but it cannot realize that potential unless it is in a flow path that allows it to intercept pollutants. Analysis of these flux pathways requires the use of advanced technologies such as models and geographic information systems (Johnston 1991a). A greater understanding of these watershed-level relationships will lead to better evaluation of wetland benefits and, ultimately, to design of watersheds for maximum wetland and surface water quality.

indirect effects of many human activities, and natural climate changes. These hydrologic alterations often severely affect biogeochemical and population processes within wetlands and lakes. For example, lakes and wetlands tend to be physically isolated and under natural conditions acquire unique biotas. However, canals and other forms of water movement between previously isolated basins increase access for invasion by exotic organisms. Invasions continue unabated throughout the United States even though the problem is widely recognized (Mills et al. 1993).

Lakes and wetlands often receive substantial physical energy and biological materials from influent streams. However, inputs of energy as well as dissolved and suspended materials entering lakes from upstream areas are altered by dams, as is the use of upstream areas for spawning fish from lakes. Likewise, heat inputs from influent streams, which modify the thermal structure, mixing, and stability of the water column and the duration of ice cover, influence basic physical, chemical, and biological processes. Variations in river inflow alter current regimes and water retention times, with concomitant changes in mixing regimes. Water level control devices common on lake outlets have similar effects. Such altered hydrologic regimes influence fringing wetlands and the organisms that depend on them for survival. For example, fishes such as northern pike depend on flooded wetlands in spring for spawning and nursery areas. In some cases, wetlands and lakes appear to be disturbance dependent, and strict water level controls are thought to degrade wetlands and shoreline habitats. Such processes are rarely understood or planned for in terms of maintaining long-term integrity of lake and wetland ecosystems. The following questions remain to be answered:

- Is it possible to develop a general model of potential ecological changes caused by hydrologic alterations that could be adapted to geomorphologically distinct lakes and wetlands?

- To what degree can artificially controlled lakes and wetlands be modified to produce predictable (and desirable) ecological systems?

Groundwater and Surface Water–Groundwater Interactions   Historically, legal, institutional, and regulatory frameworks for managing freshwater resources have been developed as if groundwater and surface waters were distinct. In fact, they are integrally connected, and movement of water between the two regimes has important ecological consequences. For example, the position of a lake in the groundwater flow field determines not only the lake's alkalinity and other chemical features but also year-to-year variability in its chemistry (Kratz et al. 1991). Changes in the ratio of precipitation inputs to groundwater inputs in a lake's water budget determine its susceptibility to acid precipitation (Anderson and Bowser 1986; Webster et al. 1990). Further, hyporheic or substream flow is now widely recognized to be an important component of many rivers and streams in supporting a unique fauna and in promoting biogeochemical interactions (Stanford and Ward 1988, 1993; Triska et al. 1989). Increasingly, groundwater is being overexploited, aquifers are collapsing, salt water is intruding, and spring and cave faunas are becoming endangered. For example, mining of water from the huge Ogallala Aquifer in the central United States has resulted in drying of wetlands and streams fed by artesian water and loss of their biotas (Cross and Moss 1987). Likewise, on the Edwards Plateau in Texas, aquifer uses by the city of San Antonio have caused extensive loss of wetlands. In the southwestern United States, groundwater withdrawals have been extremely important in the loss of many endemic fishes and molluscs (Minckley and Deacon 1991).

The importance of conserving and protecting hyporheic and other groundwater resources is at least twofold. First, pollution of deep or near-surface groundwaters may harm or destroy unique and important biological communities and thereby change or destroy the ecological processes that occur as water moves between surface waters and groundwaters. These ecological processes, many of which are microbial, are essential to maintaining high-quality freshwater ecosystems. Virtually all streams and rivers are characterized by some amount of subsurface interstitial flow. Likewise, many if not most lakes and wetlands are fed primarily by interstitial flow. Thus, the quality of drainage networks is determined largely by interactions between surface waters and groundwaters and the chemical and physical qualities of those waters. Second, groundwaters supply a large portion of the nation's potable supplies. In the United States, 40 percent of the population depends on groundwater sources for drinking water. In rural areas this figure exceeds 90 percent (General Accounting Office 1991). Much of this water is derived from near-surface aquifers, where surface waters and groundwaters interact. Indeed, subsurface interstitial flow of water has long been recognized as a natural filter that removes pollutants and provides potable water supplies for human consumption. The following questions need to be addressed:

- What are the effects of widespread changing land use on surface water–groundwater exchanges?

- How much natural purification capacity and how many endemic organisms associated with groundwaters have already been lost in the United States?

Desertification and Salinization Regulation and movement of waters often result in degradation of soil and groundwater, especially in irrigated dry regions (Williams 1981). Further, water withdrawal from aquifers adjacent to marine systems often results in saltwater incursions into fresh water. Salinization has major ecological effects that include degradation of resident biological systems and mortality of migratory birds protected under international treaties (Williams 1987). Salinization of freshwater

Table 2.3   Effects of Freshwater Resources on Human Health and Quality of Life

Component	Influence on Human Well-Being
Ecological services	Disruption of ecological systems degrades previously un-recognized services provided to human society
Drinking water quality and quantity	Supplies are being seriously depleted by withdrawals, altered runoff rates, and contamination
Aquatic food resources	Numerous toxic substances accumulate in the tissues of aquatic organisms and are eventually consumed by humans
Aesthetics and recreation	Humans manifest a variety of behaviors that illustrate the aesthetic and recreational uses and abuses of water to individuals and society
Public health	Waterborne diseases have been a major mortality factor to humans for millennia, especially when contamination is present

ecosystems is an increasing concern, especially at the regional scale. Predictive knowledge of the effects of salinization is needed if the fish and wildlife resources of these waters are to be better managed:

- How are natural characteristics of freshwater ecosystems affected by chronic changes in salinity?

- What types of organisms are replacing native biotas?

- Are all salts equally effective in changing biotas and associated ecosystem-level processes?

Threats to Human Health and Quality of Life

Freshwater resources exert an enormous influence on the health and quality of life of human populations. More than 60 percent of the world's population lives within 1 kilometer of surface water, and water is a fundamental component of our biological, economic, and social systems. Human activities, especially since 1950 (Turner et al. 1990), have significantly impaired the ability of freshwater ecosystems to provide natural ecological services, drinking water, uncontaminated food, high-quality aesthetic and recreational experiences, and controls on the spread of infectious disease (table 2.3).

Impairment of Ecological Services   Disruption of ecological systems by human activities impairs important but largely unrecognized ecological services. These include regulation of hydrologic cycles, moderation of climate extremes, absorption and detoxification of chemical contaminants, production of food, storage and cycling of essential nutrients, and provision of sites for inspiration, tourism, and recreation (Lubchenco et al. 1991). For example, riparian forests, lakeshores, and wetlands are especially important as buffers between terrestrial and aquatic systems that filter contaminants from terrestrial landscapes and maintain water quality (Naiman and Décamps 1990). Yet ecological services such as these are not comprehensively documented.

We know that aquatic systems provide real economic and social values, but these natural services remain difficult to evaluate effectively in our culture. Consider that historically society depended on natural wastewater treatment processes; that is, wastewaters were discharged into receiving bodies essentially untreated, but streams and lakes were able to assimilate and purify the wastes. However, as natural treatment capacities of water bodies were exceeded, the need to construct expensive wastewater treatment facilities expanded, at considerable cost to society. Similar difficulties exist in evaluating the role of fresh water in regulation of climate, storage and cycling of excess nutrients, detoxification of chemical and biological contaminants, and production of fish and other aquatic foods. The following questions remain:

- How can the ecological services provided by freshwater ecosystems be evaluated effectively so as to provide better judgments about their long-term value to society?

- What is required to rehabilitate the potential of fresh water to provide adequate ecological services?

Degradation of Drinking Water Quality and Quantity   Human actions have depleted water supplies by withdrawing groundwater, altering runoff rates, and contaminating surface waters and groundwaters. Nitrate, organic, and metal pollution are selected examples mentioned earlier. Drinking water supplies influence most activities of major importance to society, including human health, recreational activities, manufacturing processes, economic development, and quality of life.

Virtually all water supplies in the United States are contaminated and are potable only because of treatment to remove sediment, dangerous chemicals, and organisms and chlorination to kill microbial contaminants. For example, the Dallas–Fort Worth area in Texas obtains water from the same reservoirs that receive sewage effluents from large towns. If these municipalities did not add chlorine, 5 million people would be without drinkable water within a few hours. Many similar examples could be cited within the coterminous United States (Water Environment Federation 1992). Important concerns are as follows:

- How can the natural filtering capacity of our freshwater systems be rehabilitated in order to produce potable water?

- Can watersheds be effectively managed for water production as well as waste disposal?

Contamination of Aquatic Food Resources   Toxic substances of many kinds accumulate in tissues of aquatic organisms that are consumed by humans, such as fish, waterfowl, molluscs, water chestnuts, and wild rice. Cancer has long been a concern, and research in recent years has demonstrated some of the immunologic and reproductive effects of these contaminants (Colborn et al. 1990). Thirty-seven states had implemented fish consumption bans, restrictions, or advisories by 1989 (Reinert et al. 1991) reflecting threats to wildlife (Colborn et al. 1990) and human health (Jacobson, Jacobson, and Humphrey 1990). Complex intergenerational influences appear to include significant mental impairment of children whose mothers consume quantities of contaminated fish (Jacobson, Jacobson, and Humphrey 1990), although the generality of these conclusions is currently being examined (Dar et al. 1992). Investigation into the following areas is urgently needed:

- What are the personal and societal costs of continued contamination of freshwater food resources?

- Can we predict (or envision) the national situation ten, twenty, or even thirty years from now?

Effects on Aesthetics and Recreation   Although aesthetic values are difficult to quantify precisely, humans manifest numerous behaviors that illustrate the aesthetic value of water bodies to individuals and to society. The value of real estate adjacent to water and the number of vacations devoted to areas near water bodies demonstrate this point. The availability of expanses of clear, open water or flowing streams for humans to experience on a regular basis has profound effects on the mental and physical well-being of urban residents. This will become increasingly important if, as expected, more than 85 percent of the population resides in urban centers by the year 2050 (Berry 1990).

Recreation is already a multibillion-dollar industry, ranging from boating and fishing to hiking and swimming along rivers and water bodies of diverse sizes and shapes. Careless and poorly conceived construction (homes, boathouses, docks) seriously degrades the aesthetic value of shorelines of aquatic ecosystems. In addition, recreational values are further degraded by air, land, water, and noise pollution of aquatic resources. For example, eutrophication continues to be a serious problem in recreational uses of lakes and streams. However, complex but predictable interactions between nutrient and biotic effects on the proliferation of noxious algae provide some innovative options for water resource managers (Shapiro, Lamarra, and Lynch 1975; Carpenter 1988; Kitchell 1992). New approaches to freshwater management can succeed only if they are combined with more detailed knowledge of ecological systems and human behavior and perceptions:

- How can management of diversity, abundance, and density of organisms affect the system-level characteristics of fresh waters that are valued for aesthetics and recreation?

- What are the fundamental principles needed to maintain balance between ecological goods and services provided by fresh waters and uses of fresh waters for aesthetics and recreation?

Infectious Disease   Waterborne diseases have been a significant mortality factor for humans for millennia. Infectious disease has been reduced in the twentieth century by major efforts to treat human sewage, at least in developed countries. Problems remain in developing countries, where conditions are often unsanitary and in many cases continue to deteriorate. Infectious disease has not been eradicated and will be kept at bay only by vigilant and continuing action. In most cases the problem results from explosive population growth, conflicting demands placed on freshwater ecosystems, and inadequate interdisciplinary approaches to resolve the issues. Research is needed into the following:

- What are the environmental features of fresh water that allow for transport, transmission, and proliferation of specific waterborne diseases?

- Can those features be modified in ways that reduce infectious organisms yet maintain the overall integrity of freshwater ecosystems?

Eutrophication

Large lakes in the United States and in other parts of the world provide a broad variety of services as sources of drinking water, as deep-water fisheries, and as important recreational resources. In the second half of the twentieth century, however, many lakes lost these attributes through annual blooms of noxious cyanobacteria (Vallentyne 1974, Edmondson 1991). Runoff into regional surface waters has carried nutrients from sewage, detergents, and fertilizers as urban communities have grown and as intensified agricultural practices have been increasingly employed. Enrichment of natural lakes by these added nutrients has been a topic of considerable concern since the 1960s. Legislation at both the local and state levels has, in a number of notable instances, dramatically reduced eutrophication. Yet despite this record of success, many lakes remain seriously affected, and as populations continue to grow other freshwaters will face new or renewed pressure. Attempts to control the effects of eutrophication will require a continuing effort not only to restrict the sources of nutrients but also to widen the search for alternative approaches for nutrient disposal. These alternatives will require application of existing knowledge of the factors controlling rates of primary production and the structure of phytoplankton communities as well as continued generation of new knowledge in this area. One proposal that has received considerable study advocates manipulation of pelagic trophic structure (Shapiro, Lamarra, and Lynch 1975, Carpenter, Kitchell, and Hodgson 1985). This proposal's potential depends critically on detailed knowledge of the diversity and intensity of interactions among individual species as well as how and why interactions vary among systems. Other proposals depend on extending our knowledge of sediment chemistry or knowledge of the effects of physical mixing processes on chemical and biological dynamics. If successful, alternative approaches using limnological knowledge will provide safe and acceptable uses for excess nutrients.

Freshwater Trends In a Changing World

If issues associated with freshwater ecosystems are urgent in the United States, they are acute in other countries, seriously affecting our own national security. Water is not distributed evenly or equally among the peoples of the world. Desertification is widespread and increasing in arid and semiarid areas as a result of deficit water balances, frequently accentuated by overpopulation and overgrazing (Ehrlich and Ehrlich 1990; World Resources Institute 1990; Gleick 1993) or large-scale effects of climate change. Conflicts about availability of scarce fresh water in arid regions such as the Middle East and Africa frequently generate volatile political problems.

An International Drinking Water Supply and Sanitation Decade was launched in 1980 (Christmas and de Rooy 1991) because of dismal condi-

---

The Milwaukee Story

Waterborne diseases are a product of ineffective water resource management as well as inadequate sanitation. In 1993 some 370,000 citizens of Milwaukee, Wisconsin, were infected by an intestinal protozoan parasite, *Cryptosporidium*. Many people lost work time, and several deaths were associated with the outbreak (Edwards 1993). The contamination was traced to oocysts of the protozoan in the city's water supply, drawn from Lake Michigan. In addition, the protozoan has infected water supplies in Georgia, Texas, New Mexico, and elsewhere (Gallaher et al. 1989). For example, the Milwaukee story became the Washington, D.C., story for several days in December 1993, again due to *Cryptosporidium* contamination. Control of protozoan infections is a continuing concern within the watersheds of the reservoirs supplying the nation's large cities. Limnological knowledge and research are critical to understanding environmental controls of this pathogen, sources of the oocysts in a watershed, residence time of the oocysts in sediments, and rates of oocyst resuspension and transport to water supply intakes. Understanding of physical processes as well as biological and chemical sediment dynamics is essential.

Internationally, especially in developing countries, maintenance of water quality is critical for public health. In the 1980s, 1.2 billion people globally were without a safe water supply, with the result that more than 10 percent of the children in some population centers carried waterborne diseases (Nash 1993). Indeed, 90 percent of disease in the developing world is related to inadequate water quality (Myers 1993). Again, an understanding of the dynamics of the freshwater systems through which these diseases are transmitted is essential for maintaining water quality and human health.

---

tions relating to availability of suitable water in developing countries. Although impressive improvements in the supply of water for drinking and in sanitation services occurred in developing countries, particularly in rural areas during the 1980s, overall about 31 percent of the population in developing countries remains without potable water and 43 percent remains without sanitation services. Progress is very slow in the world's least-developed countries. In Africa, for example, only 33 percent of the rural population had a reliable supply of drinking water in 1980. This proportion had increased to only 42 percent by 1990 (Christmas and de Rooy 1991). Yet based on projected population increases, it is anticipated that more than 2 billion additional people in developing countries will require drinking water and sanitation by the year 2000 (Grover and Howarth 1991). It appears that by the year 2025, some two-thirds of the African population will be severely water stressed (Falkenmark 1989). Where will these people find sufficient water and water-based resources to survive, let alone maintain a reasonable environmental quality and standard of living?

Table 2.4   Use and Transformation of Continental Water Systems Worldwide

Alteration and Use	Year					
	1680	1800	1900	1950	1980	1985
Improved navigable waterways (km)	< 200	3,125	8,750	NA	498,000	NA
Canals (km)	5,000	8,750	21,250	NA	63,125	NA
Large reservoirs						
Number	NA	NA	41	539	NA	1,777
Volume (km^3)	NA	NA	14	528	NA	4,982
Hydropower potential (kw × 10^6)	NA	NA	NA	50	NA	550
Water withdrawal (km^3/yr × 10^3)						
Irrigation	95	226	550	1,080	NA	2,710
Consumption	5	8	25	65	195	NA
Industry and power	1	3	68	252	675	NA
All uses	104	243	654	1,415	3,640	NA
Per capita uses (m^3/yr/person × 10^3)	153	254	396	563	824	NA
Drained lands (km^2)	NA	NA	NA	NA	NA	160,600

Source: Data adapted from L'vovich and White 1990.
NA = not available.

Massive changes in the earth's freshwater systems have been occurring over the past 300 years, especially in the past 50 years. Global distribution of fresh water has changed because of human efforts to manage
the environment and because alterations to urban and rural land use have
influenced the flow and storage of water (L'vovich and White 1990). The
changes are systemically associated with a combination of rapid population growth, technological development, and lifestyle changes. For
example, per capita withdrawal of water has increased 5.4-fold in the
past 300 years, with 64 percent of that increase occurring since 1900
(table 2.4).

The extent of information about present use and anthropogenic transformations of the earth's freshwater resources allows only an approximate
description of what has happened. In L'vovich and White's (1990) reason-
ably comprehensive overview, the two most dramatic changes have been
a rapid increase in consumption since the mid-1900s and a rapid increase
in the amount of wastewater produced (table 2.4). By 1985, the volume of
polluted waters returned to rivers by industry reached nearly 600 cubic
kilometers per year, comprising 88 percent of total water intake by industry (table 2.4). In addition, increasing development of urban centers

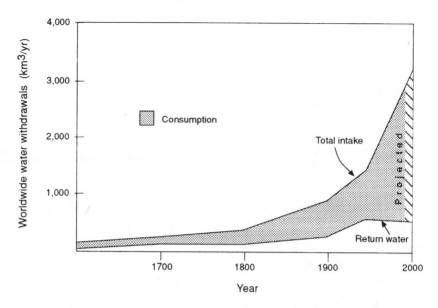

Figure 2.2 Global trends in Water Consumption by Humans and Their Technologies. Return water is the amount of water returned to the aquatic environment after use. Consumption is calculated as the difference between total intake and return water. (Adapted from L'vovich and White 1990.)

has had two major effects on water and the environment. First, domestic and industrial waste that historically might have been deposited on the soil is now channeled into rivers, lakes and reservoirs in enormous volumes through sewers and drains. Second, an increase in the area of impermeable surfaces such as roads and roofs has increased surface runoff and decreased replenishment of underground aquifers. Additionally, extensive global changes to native vegetation have altered the hydrologic cycle on a scale that is impossible to describe quantitatively.

As in the United States, withdrawal of water for irrigation and, to a lesser extent, for domestic, municipal, and industrial purposes, has caused major alterations to global water distribution (figure 2.2). The first extensive alterations of streams, beginning in the sixteenth century for navigation and power purposes, created a network of waterways. These waterways, however, did not modify stream flows greatly. Later, however, waters were accumulated through impoundments and the hydrologic regime was further altered by land management practices that drained wetlands and constricted flood flows. Collectively, these worldwide activities modified river runoff, evaporation, and the volume and amount of pollutants returned to rivers. Groundwater volumes were reduced by altered soil conditions and by direct depletion of aquifers. In addition, many large reservoirs, with distinctive aquatic environments, were created, disrupting freshwater ecosystems by stabilizing flow and isolating floods from side channels. Globally, more than 250,000 square kilometers of arid lands were converted to irrigated agricultural land and more than 160,000 square kilometers of wetlands were drained to form agricultural lands with flood protection.

In human terms, the major benefits of these physical and biological transformations of freshwater ecosystems include enhanced waterway transportation, production of electrical power, access to potable water and water for industrial processing and cooling, increased agricultural production, reduced flood hazard in some areas, and increased boating and fishing on reservoirs. Negative effects include increased flood hazard in some areas, loss of fishery resources, contamination of streams and aquifers, reduced lengths of wild rivers, loss of natural purification capacity, invasion of destabilizing exotic species such as the sea lamprey and zebra mussel, and a variety of other environmental disturbances. In many instances, development of managed water systems has supported economic growth but has also had severe environmental drawbacks.

Many major changes to freshwater ecosystems have been associated with technological innovations, especially during this century. Tools to cope with negative environmental effects of technological innovation usually follow decades later (L'vovich and White 1990). Thus, drainage typically has followed irrigation on a considerable proportion of agricultural lands. Fish ladders have been constructed only after many of the high dams were finished. Waste treatment has lagged behind sanitary sewers. Programs attempting to prevent exotic species from moving among freshwater ecosystems have been implemented only after hundreds of species have invaded. Attempts to restore goods and services provided by natural ecological systems have taken place years after the effects of water development projects were documented. If anything is to be learned from these human-induced alterations, it is that future water management must be increasingly thoughtful and innovative to prevent losses of water quality and aquatic habitat.

Freshwater Challenges in a Changing World

National and global issues associated with freshwater ecosystems will exert strong controls on the characteristics of future human societies. Five global issues will irreversibly change the earth in the near future and, in turn, profoundly affect the nation's freshwater resources. These issues are

(1) demographic patterns; (2) resource consumption; (3) environmental change; (4) shifts in institutional, social, and cultural values; and (5) utilization of information and technology. Collectively, they will produce fundamental, long-lasting changes in distribution and abundance of water resources around the world. Each issue must be acknowledged and addressed if the United States is to maintain a high-quality environment and an acceptable standard of life for its citizens.

Demographic Patterns

World population is predicted to double from its present 5.5 billion to approximately 11 billion by the year 2050. More than 90 percent of this increase is expected to occur in developing countries, where poverty and environmental degradation are most severe (Turner et al. 1990). Concomitantly, additional humanitarian demands will fall on developed countries for food, water, shelter, medicine, and fiber. In the United States, more than 85 percent of the population is expected to reside in urban centers, largely adopting urban attitudes toward water, forestry, agriculture, consumption, and the environment (Berry 1990). These attitudes include a reduced understanding of water production processes and increasingly urban-centered perceptions about commodity production in rural areas and natural ecosystem processes (Lee 1992).

Water Resource Consumption

In the United States, water consumption already is excessive. Collectively, more than 8.7 billion cubic meters of municipal and industrial effluent are discharged annually. Residues of many of the more than 80,000 human-made chemicals in common use are present in this effluent, which is enriched further by nutrients from human and agricultural waste. This is occurring at a time when demands for clean water, recreation, and fish products are doubling every one to two decades (Francko and Wetzel 1983; World Commission on Environment and Development Gore 1992).

The increasing population with its new demographic characteristics will have a substantial influence on the use and management of freshwater resources. Demand for freshwater resources will intensify, as will land use and conflicts over conservation and environmental quality. The United States can expect water supplies to be separated spatially from water consumption in the future urbanized world (Chisholm 1990). That is, water will be procured at a considerable distance from where it is consumed. The increased urban and aging components of the population (along with other factors) will contribute to changing societal values regarding the relation between human culture and water. The nation's population as a whole will probably know less about where water-based products come from and how they are produced.

Fresh water also will be a strategic resource affecting global stability. As previously discussed, great disparities exist between water consumption rates of developed and developing countries. However, as populations in developing countries expand and their quest for a higher standard of living continues, global water consumption rates are expected to increase dramatically. The available pool of water resources will decrease as a consequence, with the net impact strongly affecting the United States. Water already is extremely scarce in the Middle East and many parts of Africa; sufficient clean water is a problem for nearly all developing countries and most of the developed ones (Engelman and LeRoy 1993; Gleick 1993). Availability of water will determine the balance of political power, affecting social structures and the flow of important materials such as oil and minerals from developing countries to the rest of the world (Décamps and Naiman 1989).

Environmental Change

Present human activities will have a significant effect on the vitality of the environment well into the next century and beyond. The rate of biotic impoverishment is accelerating rapidly with the loss of species, genetic diversity, and habitat. Yet even if we choose to slow the rate of environmental change, it may not be possible to do so in the near term. Desired environmental improvements are countered by pressures of population growth in developing countries, increasing global demand for freshwater resources, and the prohibitive cost of restoration on a large scale. Existing human-caused changes in the global hydrologic cycle are leaving an environmental legacy that will affect social structures and economic functions forever, at least in human terms.

Many technological advances have made the earth a smaller place and helped overcome difficult problems relating to communication, health, and nutrition. As a result, we tend to address issues of environmental change by using technology, such as hatcheries, genetic engineering, and irrigation. However, technology cannot resolve issues unless it is applied in the context of a fundamental understanding of the character of ecological, social, and economic systems (Naiman 1992).

Institutions, Social Organizations, and Cultural Values

Institutions reflect issues of the past, not necessarily those of the future. In addition, institutions are highly resistant to change (Bennett and Dahlberg

1990). As we look to the future, with its increasingly complex, interdisciplinary issues and its inevitable new rules and regulations, the implications are clear. Massive rethinking and functional restructuring of academic and government institutions will be needed to overcome specialized divisions of labor as well as political and economic ideologies that cannot effectively address the nation's future problems.

Future tensions, however, will also come from struggles over regional, national, and international control of freshwater resources. Increasingly, controls on resource management come from outside a watershed or ecoregion. External regulatory controls result in long-term ecosystem degradation because associated environmental costs and knowledge are discounted (Turner et al. 1990). Unfortunately, the ecological literacy of local populations is poor at best; thus, national or international priorities may need to take precedence over local ones. Currently, regional control of water resources is fragmented or diminished to the point of being ineffective. A timely example of this scenario is the system of regional distribution and management of water in the western United States (Francko and Wetzel 1983).

Institutional behavior and function are important elements of any program charged with enhancing the generation and use of limnological knowledge. Science is of no use to decision makers unless effective structures exist for problem solving and decision making at the appropriate scales.

Information and Technology

More information about water resources is already available for some issues than can effectively be processed; early in the twenty-first century the volumes of data and information will be enormous. Yet without analysis and synthesis, information is not knowledge; nor is it wisdom without experienced and innovative people; nor is it useful unless it is communicated in a retrievable form. Issues often suffer from too much information, a lack of understanding as to how to apply that information, or an unwillingness to do so. Introduction of powerful computers, data management software, and remote sensing and geographic information systems will continue to assist in bridging these gaps. As environmental, social, and economic issues collide, interdisciplinary teams will be required to analyze complex sets of information and to provide effective management scenarios for policy makers and landowners to evaluate intelligently. The task of synthesizing the information and knowledge will be formidable. Will freshwater sciences and management be prepared to meet the challenge?

3

Directions for Freshwater Research

Fresh water and freshwater ecosystems are essential to the vitality and future of human societies and the environment. Research and development efforts need to be responsive to policy goals by supporting near-term decision making while developing a comprehensive understanding of the long-term dynamics of freshwater ecosystems and the complex interactions between fresh waters and human society.

National Water Issues

One of the long-term goals of freshwater research is to advance understanding of physical, chemical, and biological processes associated with fresh waters and to use that information to improve the maintenance and quality of human and environmental systems. Three national freshwater issues that in great part drive the Freshwater Imperative research agenda are as follows:

- Ecological impoverishment (degradation of aquatic ecosystem integrity), including components of habitat, biological diversity, and effects of exotic species.

- Water availability (altered hydrologic regimes), including water quality, water quantity, and timing of water-related events

- Issues related to human health and quality of life, including water-borne disease, flooding, and aesthetic values.

Although the FWI research agenda has been coupled with management and policy issues, uncertainties remain at important interfaces between science, management, and policy. These uncertainties relate to effective incorporation of research results into improved management of freshwater resources. The FWI research agenda offers recommendations coordinating research among these interfaces (see chapter 4) and for enhancing iterative cooperation among freshwater scientists, environmental managers, and policy makers.

All national water issues are expressed at regional scales in the long term. Examples are predicting effects of climate and landscape changes on freshwater ecosystems, bringing together environmental and socioeconomic scientists to pursue a joint understanding of regional freshwater problems, and focusing on solutions to regional freshwater problems through an understanding of systemic factors creating the problems. The FWI research agenda explicitly outlines the diverse political and institutional cooperation necessary to predict and respond to changes at regional scales. An integrated socioeconomic-ecological perspective at the regional scale requires institutional and interdisciplinary cooperation to a degree that has seldom been achieved in the past but that is an absolute necessity for the future.

Integrating Questions

The following questions integrate freshwater research priorities with human needs:

- What are the ecological effects of changes in the amount and routing of water and waterborne materials along the hydrologic flow path, from precipitation falling on land to the ocean, under natural and altered conditions?

- What are the effects of human activities on freshwater ecosystems, and how do they influence the sustainability of inland aquatic resources?

- Are there key features of freshwater systems that can be used to evaluate and predict the effects of human influences at regional to continental scales?

- What research infrastructure is necessary to provide effective responses to issues not yet perceived or elaborated?

These interdisciplinary questions and the national water issues presented at the beginning of this chapter were used to derive and prioritize the research areas outlined in the following FWI research agenda.

Priority Research Areas

Each of the following priority research areas is integrative, incorporating elements that are scientifically significant and socially relevant; each highlights needs for a predictive understanding of freshwater ecosystems and resources; each seeks generalizations at a regional scale for the long term; and each encourages an intensified focus on development of new paradigms in limnology. The priority research areas are, in order of importance:

1. Ecological restoration and rehabilitation

2. Maintenance of biodiversity

3. Modified hydrologic flow patterns

4. Ecosystem goods and services

5. Predictive management

6. Solution of future problems

Ecological Restoration and Rehabilitation

Regulation and management of aquatic resources in the United States have focused strongly on protection. Although this will continue, a companion effort, which is the research area of first priority, is restoration and rehabilitation of damaged or degraded systems (National Research Council 1992).

Emphasis of the research effort in ecological restoration and rehabilitation should be on providing sound scientific information, through the testing of hypotheses, to guide the reversal of ecological impoverishment. The nation's most immediate information needs center on an improved understanding of the way natural systems—from molecules to watersheds—operate in order to guide the restoration and rehabilitation efforts.

Restoration of freshwater systems to their original state will be prevented in an absolute sense by such irreversible human-caused changes as species extinction and urban expansion. In addition, humans and human settlements are an integral part of the environmental systems that are in need of restoration and rehabilitation. In most cases, watersheds and their freshwater ecosystems have been altered for decades or even centuries. Functional rehabilitation (restoring a system or creating a system similar but not equivalent to the natural one) may be the only realistic alternative to accommodate the presence of humans. System rehabilitation requires reduction of degradation, coupled with active restoration and enhancement to create displaced functions. "Rehabilitation" of freshwater ecosystems, with humans as an integral part of the systems, is perhaps a better description than "restoration" in its purest sense (Magnuson et al. 1980).

Rehabilitation can be expensive, even over small areas. Therefore, protocols must be developed for reliable assessment of feasibility. Ultimately, research in the area of restoration needs to focus on several questions, such as the following:

- Can environmental responses to specific restoration practices be predicted through a knowledge of basic processes regulating freshwater systems?

- What are the realistic environmental characteristics of a rehabilitated freshwater system that includes humans as an integral component?

Figure 3.1 illustrates the fundamental elements needed for an effective research program on freshwater restoration and rehabilitation. First, increased attention should be paid to understanding ecological vitality: how do specific freshwater ecosystems function? Aquatic ecosystems are dynamic over broad spatial and temporal scales. Long-term persistence means accepting the concepts of high interannual variation, gradually changing states, and multiple equilibria. An understanding of temporal dynamics and change in freshwater systems is important if those systems' ability to respond to changing environmental conditions is to be protected. Basic research on aquatic ecosystem components (structure and processes) provides the foundation for developing rehabilitation strategies.

Once effective strategies have been developed, experimental restoration programs can be expanded with increasing certainty of success. These experimental programs should in turn develop insights into how aquatic systems function that will further improve the nation's capability to deal effectively with freshwater issues. Restoration literally demands reassembling an ecosystem. A predictive understanding of how specific human activities, singly and in combination, affect the vitality of freshwater ecosystems provides the intellectual and practical basis for successful rehabilitation activities.

Second, an understanding is required of the causes of disturbance and degradation of freshwater ecosystems and resources and of how specific freshwater systems respond to and recover from disturbance and degradation. For example, successful restoration requires a much better understanding of the persistence and accumulation of toxic organic materials than is now available. Research should complement existing programs, such as the Environmental Protection Agency's Environmental Moni-

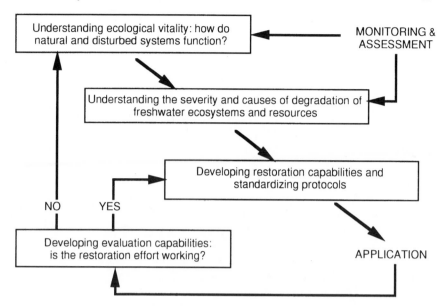

Figure 3.1.   Research Elements in Ecological Restoration and Rehabilitation

toring and Assessment Program (EMAP) and the U.S. Geological Survey's National Water Quality Assessment Program (NAWQA), which focus on inventory, monitoring, and assessment of freshwater resource conditions. Further, few long-term databases exist that can demonstrate whether statutes like the Clean Water Act and the Endangered Species Act are working as designed. The FWI research agenda strongly urges comprehensive research efforts on responses of freshwater systems to disturbance, pathways of recovery for key processes, measurement of progress toward new equilibria, and identification of environmental conditions under which systems shift to new equilibrium states.

Third, development of our nation's restoration capabilities requires, wherever appropriate, standardization of protocols across regions and habitat types. Even though rehabilitation activities are under way in a wide range of environments, in most cases they are being pursued by trial and error rather than through testing of fundamental hypotheses. A more rigorous research approach should replace these trial-and-error activities to maximize learning in a context of adaptive management (Walters 1986). Developing the range of scientifically based tools and technology required to increase the success of restoration efforts offers a timely and significant challenge to environmental scientists and engineers. For example, the most obvious engineering solutions, such as dredging of clogged river channels) may be surprisingly ineffective or may produce undesirable side

Restoration of the Degraded Kissimmee River, Florida

Beginning in 1961, a channelization project for flood control converted 166 km (103 miles) of the natural meandering channel of the Kissimmee River in central Florida into a 90 km (56 miles) canal. Excavation of the canal and associated deposition of spoil and dewatering of the floodplain destroyed 56 kilometers, or 34 percent, of the original river channel and 7,000 acres (about 2,833 hectares), or 14 percent, of the original floodplain wetlands. Habitat degradation and declining water quality generated widespread public concern over loss of natural resource values soon after the project was completed in 1971.

In 1976, the Florida legislature formed a coordinating council of state agencies with a clear and explicit mandate for restoration of water quality, water level fluctuations, and natural resource values. In addition, the Save our Rivers Act of 1981 provided funds for land acquisition, and the Surface Water Improvement and Management Act passed by the Florida legislature in 1987 provided a further mandate to move forward in restoring of the Kissimmee River watershed.

A complex pilot restoration project funded by the taxpayers of Florida through the South Florida Water Management District has demonstrated the feasibility of restoring the integrity of the combined river and floodplain ecosystems. Backfilling of the canal and installation of weirs to redirect flow from the canal into selected reaches of the old river channel are reestablishing the mosaic of habitats and destabilizing the hydrologic regime to patterns of variation that existed before channelization. As a result, habitat complexity and diversity have increased, wetland vegetation has recovered in channel and riparian areas, populations of fish and waterfowl have increased, and water quality has improved.

The success of this pilot project, along with additional modeling studies, provided the basis for implementing restoration of the Kissimmee River, including backfilling about 56 km (35 miles) of the canal. This backfilling will restore flow to the channel and reconnect the channel with its floodplain.

---

effects, such as remobilization of buried waste. Fourth, there is an important need to develop evaluation capabilities for restored systems: what metrics or objective criteria should be used to answer the questions "Is it working?" and "Is it clean enough?"

In addition, the engineering aspects of restoration must be coupled with a sophisticated understanding of the natural system in question and of fundamental system properties. Support for research into techniques and procedures for rehabilitating lakes, rivers, wetlands, and groundwaters, including rates and directions of biotic succession and reestablishment of biota and ecological processes, could not come at a more opportune time than now. Over the past fifty to two hundred years the fresh waters of the United States have undergone the most significant transformation they have experienced in nearly ten thousand years. In effect, a large human-induced experiment has been set into motion without the means to monitor its results or alter its outcome. Unless the United States develops a research infrastructure capable of addressing this issue, the trend toward ecological impoverishment of the nation's fresh waters will continue.

Maintenance of Biodiversity

Maintenance of freshwater biodiversity relates not only to diversity of species but also to diversity of ecological processes. This second priority research area has three parts:

1. Efforts to document biodiversity are hampered by a lack of baseline information for many groups of organisms and ecological processes. Current surveys and inventories delineate biodiversity for no more than about a fifth of the earth's freshwater habitats. For these surveyed habitats, only about 30 percent of the most commonly sampled benthic forms (immature stages) of insect species are identifiable because taxonomy generally is based on aerial adult forms. Fundamental survival characteristics of most species are unknown. Inferences of phylogenetic relationships are needed to predict yet-unknown characteristics of taxa from known characteristics of closely related taxa.

2. Even in regions where freshwater biodiversity is relatively well known, it is still necessary to define the importance of different species and ecological processes to human society and to ecosystem structure and function. Although the network of interactions and interdependence among microorganisms, plants, and animals is always complex, certain species and ecosystem processes influence the survival of a disproportionately large (or conspicuous) number of other species. The existence of such keystone species and critical processes suggests that survival of all species and maintenance of all processes in an ecosystem should be considered essential until the presence or absence of critical elements has been identified.

3. Even as information is gathered to document the current status and importance of freshwater biodiversity, human activities and policy decisions are posing serious, if not irreversible, threats. Effects of human activities involve (a) direct biotic manipulations, such as fish stocking and harvesting and deliberate species introductions; (b) accidental invasions by such species as the zebra mussel, Asiatic clam, and water hyacinth (*Eichhornia crassipes*); (c) physical manipulations, such as

dams, flow alterations, channelization, and water diversions; and (d) chemical inputs, such as nutrients and toxic materials. Research emphasizing the maintenance of biodiversity should be directed at baseline surveys and inventories, assessment, and biogeographic studies; specific research should focus on biotic manipulations, exotic invasions, and abiotic manipulations. Finally, evaluation of research efforts should relate to the effectiveness of applications (figure 3.2).

Apart from the service functions of taxonomy, systematics research is needed (1) to associate unknown immature benthic stages of insect species with identifiable aerial adults and (2) to infer genealogical relationships of taxa for predictive biology, providing hypotheses for yet-unknown ecological characteristics of important taxa.

Although linkages between human activities and long-term maintenance of biodiversity are clear, the nation's capacity to resolve this problem through baseline inventories and biogeographic studies is rapidly declining. Key factors limiting this area of inquiry are the training of skilled systematists with broad interests in the problems of biodiversity and the availability of molecular technologies. Unless the broad decline in systematic expertise is reversed, the United States soon will not be able to

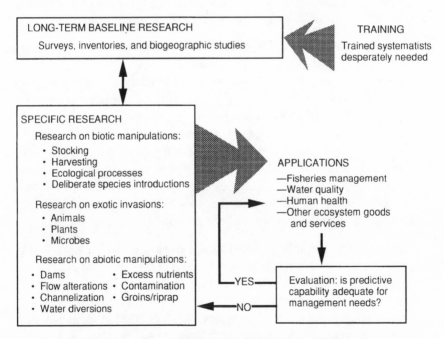

Figure 3.2.   Research Elements in Maintenance of Biodiversity

Maintaining Biodiversity

Evidence of biological impoverishment is pervasive in aquatic systems. The threat to aquatic biodiversity is more serious than threats to terrestrial diversity or even the integrity of tropical rainforests. From 11 to 15 percent of terrestrial vertebrates (birds, mammals, and reptiles) in the United States are classed as rare to extinct, while the proportion of aquatic biota similarly classed ranges from 34 percent for fish to 65 percent for crayfishes and 75 percent for unionid mussels (Master 1990). Of 214 stocks of Pacific salmon, 74 percent have a high or moderate risk of extinction (Nehlsen, Williams, and Lichatowich 1991).

Conservatively, 20 percent of the world's freshwater fish are extinct or in serious decline (Moyle and Leidy 1992). Despite massive expenditures to improve water quality, none of 251 fishes listed as rare in 1979 were removed from the list in 1989 because of successful recovery efforts (Williams et al. 1989). Some have, however, been removed by extinction, such as the Tecopa pupfish (*Cyprinodon*). In major U.S. river systems, commercial harvesting of fishes has declined by at least 80 percent (Karr 1993), and in some cases the decline has approached nearly 100 percent.

Reduction in diversity of native bivalve molluscs (Mollusca, order Unionioda) and fishes (Pisces) by human actions is expected to continue. There are 297 taxa of bivalves north of Mexico; of these, 18 taxa are presumed extinct, 44 species are listed or proposed as federally endangered, and another 69 species may be endangered (Bogan 1995). Collectively, extinct and endangered bivalve taxa represent 44 percent of the native fauna. This massive loss of bivalve diversity can be traced to impoundment and inundation of riffle habitat in major river systems, such as the Ohio, Tennessee, Cumberland, and Mobile Bay, and loss of the bivalve's host fish species.

More than one factor has contributed to the decline and extinction of 82 percent of the fishes. Alteration of physical habitat is the most frequently cited (73 percent), followed by detrimental effects of introduced species (68 percent), chemical alteration of habitat (38 percent), hybridization (38 percent), and overharvesting (15 percent) (Miller et al. 1989). Unionid bivalves are very long-lived (30–130 years), as are fish (1–25 years), so effects on a species may not be immediately detectable.

Even though it is well known that these losses are largely a direct result of habitat loss and fragmentation, they deserve special mention because of their economic and social values and because the many secondary causes of decline—invasion by exotic species, effects of pollutants, and harvest strategies—are poorly understood. Other manifestations of continuing degradation include declining genetic diversity, often exacerbated by ill-conceived programs, such as salmon hatcheries in the Pacific Northwest (Meffe 1992), and an annual average of forty states issuing fish consumption advisories (Reinert et al. 1991).

address many of the biodiversity issues relating to fresh waters (Systematics Agenda 2000 1994).

Biotic manipulations of freshwater ecosystems relate directly to management activities in fisheries. Stocking and harvesting of fish and other freshwater organisms need to be compatible with existing native biodiversity and biological processes. Resolution of this problem requires identifying species and ecological processes most affected by stocking and harvesting and investigating processes that regulate targeted populations. Research is needed to identify sensitive species—which will vary with the type of freshwater system and ecoregion—and to develop general approaches to investigating this problem at scales beyond a small group of sites or species. In addition, an understanding of the long-term effects of fisheries management on broader ecosystem processes is essential for maintaining the integrity of freshwater systems.

An understanding of the effects of invading exotic organisms on freshwater ecosystems is also of high priority. The knowledge required relates primarily to predicting probable success and effects, both positive and negative, of potential invaders or introduced species and identifying the characteristics of aquatic sites that make them susceptible to invasion. Interactions between invading and native species and the temporal scales over which these interactions occur are the keys to such an inquiry. Questions include the following:

- What traits of invaders allow them to become established?

- Are there functional types of freshwater species that are especially capable of invading?

- Are some communities more resistant to invasion? If so, why?

- Why are there differences in invasiveness and susceptibility to invasion?

- What are the principle vectors of dispersal, and can these vectors be managed?

Although these and other questions in this research area are contemporary in nature, the answers are rooted in classical community ecology. New research is needed to carry these questions to larger spatial and temporal scales so that dispersal and subsequent effects of invading species can be predicted for a variety of aquatic systems. In particular, comparative field studies of communities are needed both in advance of and behind invasion fronts in light of the rate of global environmental change.

Some invasions are the result of intentional human manipulation to increase economic productivity. For example, in North America the introduction of game fishes such as salmon (*Oncorhynchus* spp.), bass (*Micropterus* spp.), and walleye have greatly affected native species and aquatic ecosystems (Carpenter 1988; Carpenter and Kitchell 1993). Accidental invasions are a second but equally important consequence of human activities on biodiversity. The recent accidental introduction of the zebra mussel via ballast water from intercontinental shipping into North America may lead to widespread local extinctions of native molluscs as well as hundreds of millions of dollars' worth of damage to water intake systems around the Great Lakes (Ludyanskiy, McDonald, and MacNeil 1993). The nearly simultaneous appearance of the predatory cladoceran *Bythotrephes* has altered the zooplankton community intermediate in the food chain of the Great Lakes (Sprules, Reissen, and Jin 1990; Lehman 1991). These are only a few of the hundreds of exotic introductions taking place each decade in the nation's fresh waters.

Biodiversity is strongly influenced by physical and chemical manipulations that affect organisms either directly or through disruption of their habitat. Physical manipulations of water flow occur because of societal needs for fresh water in municipalities, agriculture, industry, and power generation. Future effects on water flow are likely to result from climate change. Changes in flow disrupt the hydrologic cycle and the hydraulics of water movement and consequently alter the life histories and productivity of freshwater species. An understanding of the effects of alterations in water flow on the maintenance of species and community structure is essential for effective management. The ecological sciences should incorporate a deeper appreciation of the role of physical factors such as turbulence, geomorphic structure, boundary layer shear stress, and advective processes in regulating population dynamics. There is a critical need to link physical and biological processes at appropriate scales to understand how physical variability influences biodiversity. Likewise, chemical characteristics also influence biodiversity. For example, when freshwater ecosystems are enriched with nutrients such as nitrogen and phosphorus, species adapted to lower-nutrient environments are replaced by species able to utilize higher nutrient concentrations. Further, biodiversity is affected by pesticides and herbicides, acid precipitation, and contamination by a wide variety of organic and inorganic materials. We also know little of the natural rates of species turnover and persistence in aquatic systems (Magnuson , Benson, and McLain 1994). Can a series of general models be developed, based on type of manipulation or on life history characteristics of the organisms, that allow reliable predictions of species persistence in a changing environment? If so, these comprehensive models, developed through research on maintaining biodiversity, should help build a predictive capability for effective management.

Modified Hydrologic Flow Patterns

Water flow is critical for ecosystem functioning. The third priority of understanding the long-term effects of modified hydrologic regimes on environmental systems requires integrating the disciplines of hydrology and physical limnology—one emphasizing flow into aquatic ecosystems; the other, flow within systems. Emphasis should be on defining physical processes operating on and within the ecological system. Two fundamental questions related to modified hydrologic regimes are as follows:

- What are the ecological effects of changes in amount and routing of water, waterborne materials, and organisms along the hydrologic flow path from precipitation to the ocean under natural and altered conditions?

- What are the consequences of altered thermal regimes due to modified hydrologic regimes on ecological processes and community structure within freshwater ecosystems?

There are, of course, numerous indirect effects of human activities on hydrologic regimes. Although lakes, wetlands, streams, and groundwater along the flow path all experience the direct effects of climate and land use impacts, downstream systems experience indirect effects through changes in inputs of water, nutrients, organic matter, and other materials from upstream. Over time these changes alter the physical, chemical, and biotic structure and function of the downstream ecosystems. The evolving watershed then has a different set of interactions with humans and with the earth. For example, exchanges of "greenhouse" gases between the watershed and atmosphere are altered as wetlands change, while yields of mammals and fish to humans are changed as plant species composition and productivity shift to new ecological states.

Addressing the fundamental hydrologic questions requires integrated physical, chemical, and biological research on disturbances affecting all components of the hydrologic flow path, including movement of water through the soil and into shallow groundwater and exchanges of shallow groundwater with the network of wetlands, lakes, reservoirs, and streams. Human activities have altered the amount and routing of water along these flow paths. Increases in irrigation and other diversions reduce water flow in channels; construction of dams offers barriers to water movement and affects the character of upstream and downstream ecosystems; and

Ecological Effects of Changing Hydrology on Lakes

Changes in depth and morphology of lakes follow variations in annual precipitation, increased melting of glaciers, and changes in land use. As a consequence, mixing patterns within affected lakes are altered, as are the lakes' biological communities. For example, increased freshwater inputs to hypersaline Mono Lake during the El Niño Southern Oscillation of the 1980s reduced vertical mixing and decreased the flux of ammonium to the euphotic zone. Resulting decreases in phytoplankton concentrations in the spring led to reduced densities of zooplankton and to changes in age structure of the zooplankton population during the summer. A similar phenomenon caused by melting of glaciers in the Antarctic beginning in the 1980s has increased freshwater inputs to lakes there, triggering a sequence of events similar to those in Mono Lake: when inflowing waters are fresher than the lake waters, reduced vertical mixing occurs, altering biogeochemical cycling of elements, microbial processes, and dynamics of the biological community.

In another example, the depth of lakes in the Amazon River floodplain varies seasonally with riverine input. When a lake's level is low, its entire water column mixes diurnally, stirring bottom sediments and raising the lake's turbidity. As the water level rises, complete mixing becomes less frequent and finally ceases. A difference in depth of only about one meter determines whether a lake will mix to its bottom or to only a part of its depth. Once a lake no longer mixes to the depths of its sediments, the biomass of phytoplankton above the diurnal thermocline increases, water below the thermocline becomes anoxic, and methane concentrations increase. These changes in mixing regime affect particle movement and nutrient flux, with significant consequences for lake productivity.

These examples indicate the importance of vertical mixing to the productivity of lakes and show how alterations in water flow can disrupt existing patterns. Although reductions in vertical mixing due to increased inputs of freshwater to most lakes may not be as extreme as in the salt lakes mentioned earlier, it is known that mixing patterns of lakes can be greatly altered by modifications in the watershed. Anoxic periods in the bottom water can be extended substantially not only by eutrophication, which leads to greater decomposition of dead organisms on the lake bottom, but also by direct input of salts. Road salt, used to inhibit ice formation in the winter in many north-temperate cities, frequently drains into lakes, where it can create a layer of slightly saline bottom water that resists mixing (Bubeck et al. 1971). Here decomposition products accumulate and oxygen is depleted, with distinct ramifications for water quality and ecological processes. Additionally, road construction and maintenance have been shown to cause currents of high-density clay-laden water that can destabilize stratification patterns, again with potentially dramatic effects on ecological processes (Culver 1975; Culver et al. 1981).

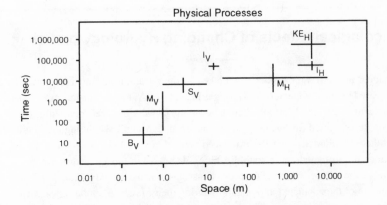

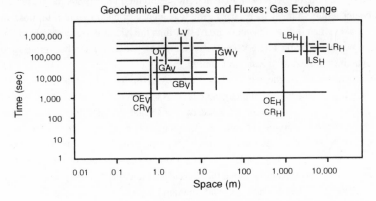

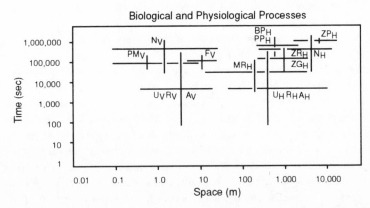

Figure 3.3. Spatial and Temporal Scales of Limnological Processes Estimated for Lake Biwa, Japan, for a Typical Month in Late Summer. This analysis was used to help design BITEX, an international interdisciplinary study of biological, chemical, and physical processes in Lake Biwa organized by the Lake Biwa Research Institute (Otsu, Japan) and the Center for Water Research (Perth, Australia). The key to symbols, the direction of influence, and the spatial and temporal scales of the process are given on the facing page (Adapted from J. Melack, J. Catalon, and R. Oliver, unpublished data.).

Process	Direction	Spatial Scale	Temporal Scale
Physical Processes			
Billows (in thermoclines) (B_V)	Vert.	0.1–1.0 m	10–60 sec.
Seiche (S_V)	Vert.	1–10 m	1–4 h.
Kelvin wave and eddy formation (KE_H)	Horiz.	1–10 m	1–10 d.
Intrusions (I_H)	Horiz.	2–3 km	1 h.–1 d.
Intrusions (I_V)	Vert.	10–20 m	0.5–1 d.
Upper mixed layer (including wind-driven current) M_V	Vert.	0.1–10 m	1 min.–1 h.
Upper mixed layer (MH)	Horiz.	0.01–10 km	1 h.–1 d.
Geochemical Processes and Fluxes			
Solute and particle supply			
Streams (LS_H)	Horiz.	0.5–10 km	1–10 d.
Rain (LR_H)	Horiz.	5–10 km	1–2 d.
Sediments (LB_H)	Horiz.	1–10 m	0.5–10 d.
All (L_V)	Vert.	0.1–10 m	0.5–10 d.
Inorganic particle sedimentation (O_V)	Vert.	0.1–40 m	2 h.–10 d.
Desorption and adsorption (OE_H)	Horiz.	0.1–10 km	1 min.–1 d.
Desorption and adsorption (OE_V)	Vert.	0.1–10 m	1 min.–1 d.
Speciation changes (chelation, complexing, and redox) (CR_H, CR_V)	Horiz. + vert.	As for desorption/adsorption	
Gas Exchange			
Air-water (GA_V)	Vert.	0.1–10 m	1 min.–1 d.
Sediment-water (GB_V)	Vert.	0.1–40 m	1 h.–10 d.
Water column (GW_V)	Vert.	0.1–40 m	1 h.–2 d.
Biological Processes			
Phyto/bacterial net growth (PP_H, BP_H)	Horiz.	0.2–3 km	2–10 d.
Zooplankton net growth (ZP_H)	Horiz.	2–10 km	7–10 d.
Grazing clearing rate (ZG_H)	Horiz.	0.2–5 km	2 h.–2 d.
Nutrient regeneration zooplankton (ZR_H)	Horiz.	Equal to grazing scales	
Microbial regeneration (MR_H)	Horiz.	0.01–5 km	1 h.–1 d.
Plankton movement (PM_V)	Vert.	0.1–10 m	0.5–2 d.
Fecal pellets (F_V)	Vert.	10–40 m	0.5–2 d.
Physiological Processes			
Photoadaptation (A_V)	Vert.	1–40 m	1 min.–2 d.
Photoadaption (A_H)	Horiz.	0.05–10 km	1 min.–2 d.
Respiration (R_V)	Vert.	1–40 m	1 min.–2 d.
Respiration (R_H)	Horiz.	0.05–10 km	1 min.–2 d.
Cellular pools (N_V)	Vert.	0.1–40 m	1 h.–10 d.
Cellular pools (N_H)	Horiz.	0.05–10 km	1 h.–10 d.
Nutrient uptake (UV + UH)	Vert. + horiz.	As for photoadaption	

channelization restricts lateral and vertical exchanges in streams. These direct manipulations not only influence exchange of materials but also profoundly affect habitability for freshwater biotas.

The characteristics of aquatic ecosystems are directly influenced by changes in subsurface and surface inflows (typically the province of hydrologists) and by changes in inputs of solar energy and momentum (typically the province of physical limnolog:sts). Changes in these factors affect stratification, current regimes, and horizontal and vertical mixing within a water body. In turn, changes in these processes affect the variety and persistence of habitats within lakes, streams, and wetlands as well as processes such as nutrient cycling, photosynthesis, dispersion of larvae, reproductive success, and predator-prey interactions.

Long-term and comparative research on modified hydrologic regimes should address flow characteristics of streams, lakes, and groundwater; precipitation and evapotranspiration; sediment and nutrient loads; geochemical features; effects of changing surface energy budgets on flow patterns; manipulative studies of the effects of land use activities and climate change on specific hydrologic parameters; comparisons of natural and highly modified watersheds; and studies of physical limnological parameters in restored watersheds (see, for example, figure 3.3).

Unfortunately, the effects of watershed alterations on hydrologic regimes are highly complex and not always predictable (table 2.2). Use of landscape- or watershed-scale approaches (for example, Hubbard Brook Experimental Forest, Coweeta Hydrological Laboratory, J. H. Andrews Experimental Forest, and others) comparing hydrologic parameters across highly altered and less modified watersheds, will continue to be valuable in assessing effects. However, new long-term watershed research programs should be established, and existing programs enhanced, in additional ecoregions of the United States and where environmental change includes agricultural, power production, and urban alterations. Relating land use activities to other physical characteristics (such as slope and geology) and ecological features (such as vegetative cover and soil type) will aid in assessment of various physical alterations on erosion, sedimentation, water storage, and other hydrologic parameters. Experimental and human-induced manipulations at a wide range of spatial and temporal scales will be essential in understanding the effects of specific watershed alterations on hydrologic responses.

The status and trends of landscape patterns within watersheds across ecoregions of the United States also need to be quantified (figure 3.4). Applications of remote sensing and geographic information system (GIS) technology can be used to address questions regarding spatial patterns of land use, to define and determine the extent of various landscape alterations, and to evaluate changes in landscape patterns over time (including land use, fragmentation, and changes in connectivity of isolated lakes, ponds, and wetlands) on the hydrologic cycle.

Understanding and predicting effects of modified hydrologic regimes ultimately requires accurate responses to questions such as the following:

- How do altered hydrologic regimes affect biotic diversity and biotic interactions in freshwater systems?

- How do altered hydrologic regimes affect riparian and other down-stream ecosystems (groundwater and overland flow drainage systems)?

- How do altered hydrologic and physical limnological regimes affect biogeochemical cycling and movement of nutrients, chemicals, particles, and organisms through freshwater ecosystems and their associated landscapes and airsheds?

In the end, however, a significant aspect of this research program will be the evaluative research that determines whether predictive capability is adequate for managerial needs (figure 3.4). As the nation attempts to restore degraded aquatic systems, it is critical that restoration of the natural hydrologic flow path be one of the first steps (National Research Council

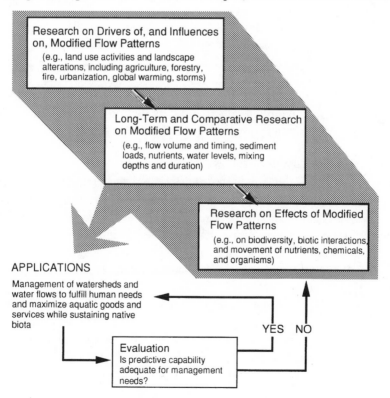

Figure 3.4.   Research Elements in Modified Hydrologic Flow Patterns

---

Hubbard Brook Experimental Forest

Sustained ecological research on the flux of water and chemicals from precipitation through forest and associated aquatic ecosystems within the Hubbard Brook Experimental Forest, New Hampshire, has provided significant insights into ecological systems (Likens 1992). It was here that acid rain was discovered in North America. Also, using powerful experimental manipulations of entire watersheds, effects of various forestry practices on water yield and quality, as well as on rates of forest regrowth, were determined. This sustained research program has generated important insights into such ecosystem functions as evapotranspiration, dry deposition, and weathering—parameters that are difficult to quantify in ecosystems. Integration of long-term data on these features, as well as on precipitation, stream water chemistry, and hydrology, and characterization of the dynamics of atmospheric gases and water within the system, showed how the watershed moderates inputs and how its outputs affect biogeochemical cycles.

Current federal protocols for timber harvesting in the northeastern United States are rooted in the results from Hubbard Brook. A major finding from the watershed experiments there is that forest cutting can dramatically disrupt an ecosystem's nitrogen cycle and cause large quantities of nutrients, including nitrate, to move from the disturbed landscape into drainage water. Not only can these losses be significant for the terrestrial ecosystem, but they can also cause major inputs of nutrients into downstream freshwater systems.

1992). If properly designed, such restoration efforts offer to limnologists the potential for manipulative experiments that will advance our understanding of how human activities affect freshwater ecosystems.

Ecosystem Goods and Services

Human influences on aquatic systems cannot be avoided and, in fact, should be anticipated (McDonnell and Pickett 1993). However, use of aquatic ecosystems should be guided by the principle of sustainability (World Commission on Environment and Development 1987), which implies that the goods and services are provided by ecosystems should be protected, restored, and enhanced where possible. This is the fourth priority research area.

Candidates for such a management approach would be major U.S. river systems, where commercial harvesting of fishes has declined by at least 80 percent (Karr 1993). Harvest in the Illinois River has declined by nearly 100 percent during this century (Karr, Toth, and Dudley 1985), while populations of migratory salmon in the Columbia River have declined by more than 95 percent (excluding hatchery runs—Ebel et al. 1989). Harvest in the Missouri River has decreased by 85 percent since 1945 (Hesse et al. 1989), and that in Delaware River has decreased by a similar amount (Patrick 1992). Additional resources have been decimated as well (for example, migratory birds, especially waterfowl—Bellrose 1980).

Emphasis in this priority research area is on a better understanding of environmental goods and services provided by freshwater ecosystems: (1) water quantity and quality, (2) biological productivity, and (3) aesthetics and recreation (figure 3.5). These research topics are considered briefly on the following pages. Although it is not specifically addressed in this chapter, an understanding of human culture, values, and institutions must be integrated with research results to provide for effective management of the water and watersheds that supply freshwater goods and services. Continual evaluation will be necessary to determine the effectiveness of management applications of research results (figure 3.5). Important questions are as follows:

- Can present levels of goods and services be sustained or increased in a sustainable manner?

- How can information on resources, system productivity, and aesthetics and recreation be integrated so as to provide for sustainable use and management of freshwater goods and services?

Water Quality and Quantity Water quality is defined by concentrations of dissolved and suspended substances. Throughout the United States, water quality is almost infinitely variable because of the large

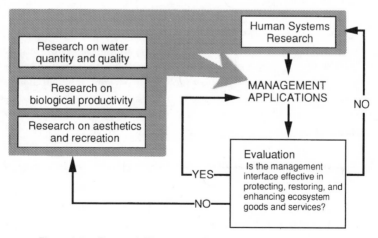

Figure 3.5. Research Elements in Ecosystem Goods and Services

Nitrogen in Estuaries

Eutrophication continues to be a problem in many coastal waters and estuaries, including Chesapeake Bay, New York Bight, and Chowan Basin (summarized by Nixon et al. 1986). Increased nutrient loads stimulate phytoplankton production and alter species composition. Eutrophication may also increase toxic algal blooms (Anderson, Galloway, and Joseph 1992) and cause dieback of submerged grass beds. Oxidation of inflowing nutrients and decomposition of the increased phytoplankton biomass deplete available oxygen and may result in anoxic conditions. Anoxic and hypoxic waters cause appreciable damage to finfish and shellfish resources.

The primary cause of eutrophication varies with the estuarine system (Nixon and Pilson 1983). The major contributing nutrient depends on the quantity and composition of river inputs to the estuary, physical characteristics of the estuary, and the importance of nitrogen fixation and internal nutrient recycling (Jawarski 1981, Nixon 1981). Nitrogen generally is the nutrient most limiting to phytoplankton growth during the peak growing season in most temperate estuaries. Sources of nitrogen vary from system to system but include sewage, agricultural runoff, fertilizer from suburban lawns, and atmospheric deposition. As an example, nitrogen inflow from wastewater discharges ranged from 32 percent in the Chesapeake Bay to 63 percent in the Hudson River. Watershed runoff containing nitrogen from urban and agricultural land uses can account for 18 percent (New York Bay) to 99 percent (Barataria Bay) of the total nitrogen load. Atmospheric deposition appears to be a major source of nitrogen in many estuaries, although its exact magnitude is poorly known.

Numerous factors regulate the flow of nitrogen from watershed to estuary, including geomorphology of the watershed, hydrology, soils, and land use. Impervious surfaces such as parking lots and clearing of land for agriculture greatly increase water flow and nitrogen loads to estuaries. On the other hand, processes such as retention by soils, uptake by riparian vegetation, and loss through denitrification in wetlands, streams, and rivers can decrease nitrogen transport to the estuary. These processes are complex and have strongly interacting biological, chemical, and physical components. As an example, losses of nitrogen via denitrification are determined by location, width, vegetation, and hydrology of riparian forests and wetlands.

To deal adequately with the growing problem of estuarine eutrophication, we must understand the regulation of nitrogen flows to estuaries from all major sources. This will require interdisciplinary research by those with expertise in hydrology; in atmospheric, soil, estuarine, and forest sciences; and in geography, geology, ecology, and planning as well as in aquatic sciences.

number of substances carried and the great variety of physical and chemical forms in which substances can be transported. The range of effects that dissolved and suspended substances have on freshwater ecosystems extends from metabolic stimulation to toxicity, and when introduced concurrently these substances can have powerful cumulative effects on the biota.

In addition, since effects may show great qualitative variation across a range of concentrations, an understanding of water quality in relation to ecosystem characteristics is needed for both natural and modified aquatic ecosystems. Important related issues include toxic substances, nutrients, sediments, and organic inputs. Research should focus on cumulative effects of multiple contaminants because ecosystem-level effects cannot be predicted from studies of single contaminants.

Toxic substances, including metals, herbicides, and industrial chemicals, are pervasive in almost all freshwater systems. The nation's use of toxic materials has created a pressing set of questions for scientists, resource managers, and regulators:

- Can specific toxins be ranked in priority of importance from a perspective that encompasses not only human health but also environmental damage and indirect effects?

- What are the processes by which various categories of toxic substances are routed through and metabolized by freshwater ecosystems?

- How can contaminated systems be restored following toxification?

- Are there fundamental mechanisms influencing the cumulative effects of introduction of multiple types of chemicals, sediment, and organic matter?

These questions are best approached through an ecosystem perspective—from the perspective of entire systems—with consideration of multiple temporal and spatial scales as well as numerous trophic and chemical pathways.

Nutrients have powerful multiplier effects on aquatic systems and are transferred to fresh waters in large amounts by human activity (figure 3.6). For example, 1 kilogram (2.2 pounds) of phosphorus added to a lake or stream may cause the growth of as much as 1,000 kilograms (2,200 pounds) of plant biomass. Since nutrient mobilization is often linked to land use, prediction of the effects of land use on freshwater systems must be based on a firm understanding of the mechanisms by which aquatic systems respond to nutrient additions. Research questions include the following:

- How can rates of nutrient mobilization be estimated and modeled regionally for specific land use patterns?

- What are the natural pathways of nutrient fluxes both inside and outside freshwater ecosystems?

- What are the mechanisms by which human activities distort material pathways?

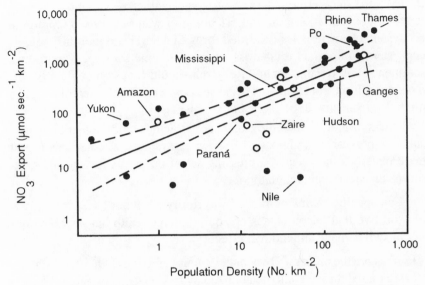

Figure 3.6.   Relationship Between Nitrate Export from Selected Rivers and Human Population Density of Watersheds. Open circles represent tropical rivers. Solid line is least-squares regression; dashed lines are 95 percent confidence interval for regression (Adapted from Cole et al. 1993).

- How can the sensitivity and response spectrum of freshwater systems to nutrient loading be anticipated?

- What are the key environmental factors that control the frequency, intensity, and duration of responses?

Sediments are also mobilized by land use practices such as road construction, agriculture, and urban development. Although some effects of sediment can be studied through water quality and nutrient investigations, others involve physical alteration of aquatic systems in ways that are just now being understood (Terrene Institute 1993). The following, and many other fundamental questions, require responses for effective management applications:

- How are the pathways of water flow at small spatial scales affected by fine sediments, and what are the consequences for organisms and for system productivity?

- How are freshwater habitats physically reconfigured by sediment transport?

- What are the biological consequences of sedimentation on breeding and nursery areas or refuges?

- How do sediments affect the quantity and availability of nutrients or toxins?

- How do sediment characteristics change the availability and quality of light for primary producers and affect stratification in the water column?

- How do changing flow patterns and thermal regimes affect settling and resuspension of sediments?

Organic matter enters freshwater environments by natural pathways, including runoff and groundwater flow. However, human activities frequently cause large increases of organic inputs through sewage disposal or agriculture that significantly alter or disrupt aquatic ecosystem functions. The following issues need to be investigated:

- What amounts of organic matter enter various kinds of freshwater systems under natural conditions?

- How is this organic matter processed and utilized in the aquatic system?

- How much augmentation of the organic load can different types of freshwater systems sustain before they are significantly altered?

The quantity of water reaching freshwater environments varies on time scales ranging from hours to decades or more (see the section on modified hydrologic flow patterns earlier in this chapter). Quantity of flow is perhaps the most extensively manipulated of all variables affecting aquatic systems and represents a strong and continuous linkage between water bodies and land use (Petts 1984; Naiman and Décamps 1990). Natural and anthropogenic variation of flow regimes regulates biotic production, material fluxes, and community composition of aquatic environments. Although many effects of altered flow are potentially predictable, they are not sufficiently understood in relation to their fundamental or practical importance. Quality and quantity of water are closely connected because water flow often controls mobilization or dilution of dissolved and suspended substances. It is unrealistic to study water quality and quantity separately, especially as they relate to transport and dilution of toxic chemicals, nutrients, sediments, and organic matter. Research is needed in the following areas:

- Are there hydrologic thresholds below which the freshwater ecosystem is severely degraded or altered?

- What are the natural features of aquatic ecosystems that affect water flow (such as riparian forests), and how can they be managed to maintain water flow and other environmental attributes?

Biological Productivity   There are a number of general research frontiers in the area of biological productivity, including (1) factors limiting
heterotrophic production by microbes and other microinvertebrates, (2)
biophysical transformations that limit and influence productivity in riparian and wetland ecotones between land and water, (3) the quality of
food resources and ways in which food quality influences community
structure and pathways of material flow, (4) the role of food web structure
in determining biological productivity and vice versa, and (5) environmental lag times and life history controls within populations that affect
community structure and dynamics.

Although it is known that microbial and microinvertebrate heterotrophic
production is frequently limited by availability of nutrients and carbon in
freshwater systems, important questions remain unresolved. For example,
there is no general community-level understanding of how changes in
shear stress, turbulence, or mixing regimes of fresh waters influence the
production of microbes, protozoa, and other invertebrates. Further, in
carbon-limited systems, it is still not possible to predict changes in community composition or productivity with increasing turbidity following
sediment input from a watershed. Apparently simple alterations continue
to have complex environmental responses.

Transformation of nutrients and retention of sediment and other materials at land-water margins (ecotones) are important because fluxes across
and retention of materials within riparian zones, floodplains, and littoral
zones strongly influence the biotic characteristics of freshwater ecosystems (Naiman et al. 1988; Gregory et al. 1991; Stanford and Ward 1993).
Major questions remain concerning the relative significance of land-water
ecotones in determining biological productivity at the watershed scale.
For example, ecotones may harbor critical life stages of some species, providing refuges from predation and resources for growth. However, it is not
possible to predict quantitatively the direct and indirect effects of reduction in this habitat on overall watershed-level productivity. Riparian forest
ecotones also offer valuable management tools for reducing nutrient
loading in streams and lakes and for maintaining biodiversity; basic ecological studies are needed to optimize their design (Pinay et al. 1990;
Naiman, Décamps, and Pollock 1993).

The influence of food quality, as measured by chemical composition
and metabolic activity, is a key subject in the future integration of population biology and ecosystem science, and has strong implications for management of freshwater ecosystems. Each species of consumer differs in its
chemical composition—that is, the ratios of carbon to nitrogen to phosphorus and other elements. Consumers acquire in their diet the appropriate

mix of elements to sustain growth: elements in short supply are retained while others are more rapidly recycled. This "stoichiometric" interaction of consumer populations and biogeochemical cycles (Sterner, Elser, and Hessen 1992; Sterner 1994) is fundamental to determining the characteristics of freshwaters. Yet subtle chemical alterations have strong environmental effects that are almost impossible to predict even theoretically.

A significant advance has been the recent discovery of how food web structure influences biological productivity. Productivity and biomass of distinct constituents of an aquatic ecosystem are partly determined by predation forces from the top of the food web (Hrbacek et al. 1961; Carpenter, Kitchell, and Hodgson 1985; Wootton and Power 1993). Conversely, the influence of primary productivity in constraining trophic structure from the bottom of the food web appears equally important (Sterner, Elser, and Hessen 1992; Sterner 1994). Further questions remain to be answered:

- What are the relative importance and level of interaction between these two opposing forces in different types of freshwater ecosystems?

- Can appropriate application of the resulting knowledge continue to provide substantial improvement in management of fisheries and water quality in all types of freshwater ecosystems?

Harvesting of freshwater resources is often limited by reproductive recruitment. There are important linkages between human activities and successful recruitment and harvesting of commercial species. Increased harvesting often causes variability in recruitment and shifts in community structure (Miller et al. 1988; Levin 1993; Ludwig, Hilborn, and Walters 1993). In addition, forecasting the recruitment of commercial freshwater resources is especially challenging in the context of global environmental change.

These are only some examples of basic needs in the study of biological productivity. Although in some cases rates of biological productivity can be predicted, the ability to make successful predictions is limited at important temporal and spatial scales. For instance, forecasting the development of toxic algal blooms means understanding processes regulating the growth and mortality of toxic algae, including significant interactions among turbulence, nutrient cycling, and grazing (Anderson, Galloway, and Joseph 1992). Issues related to maintaining acceptable levels and types of biological productivity in the nation's freshwaters will require interdisciplinary research, new manipulative research sites, professional education, and sustained cooperation between freshwater sciences and management.

Aesthetics and Recreation   Quantification of aesthetic and recreational values associated with freshwater resources is important because of their effects on human health and quality of life. In addition to quantification of direct user values, research should also focus on further development and application of contingent valuation, or nonuser values. Utilization of user and nonuser value methodologies could, in many cases, provide useful information to decision makers and resource managers when considering the long-term consequences of proposed water resource plans, such as housing developments, shoreline structures, and power plants. Of particular importance are research activities related to establishing carrying capacities in heavily used recreational areas and in natural areas (that is, answering the question "How many people is too many people?"); determining the environmental effects of new water-based recreational activities (for example, rafting and sailboarding); managing regulated rivers in terms of meeting the needs of recreational river user (for example, providing river flows for whitewater rafting); and providing fish that meet the needs of the fishing public while protecting biological integrity. To be realistic, the research identified here requires a durable partnership between social and freshwater scientists.

Predictive Management

The FWI research agenda identifies as its fifth research priority significant areas of uncertainty that can be reduced by targeted research over the next decade. Ecological predictions will always be uncertain, and quantitative estimates of uncertainty will always be necessary for environmental decision making. However, there is an opportunity to improve substantially the nation's capacity to predict changes in freshwater ecosystems driven by management, human-induced stress, and environmental change.

Uncertainties at three levels frustrate ecologists and resource managers (Hilborn 1987). (1) Noise is variability that occurs frequently enough to be routine. Scientists and managers expect noise and cope with it through sampling schemes and statistical analyses. (2) Unknown but potentially knowable states of nature are a more intriguing type of uncertainty. These are the uncertainties that scientists hope to reduce through research. (3) Surprises are events that are not anticipated. Although specific surprises cannot be forecast (by definition), it is certain that some surprises will occur. Flexible, adaptive management schemes cope with surprise more effectively than do rigid, dogmatic ones.

Predictive capabilities are essential to moving management sciences from a reactive mode, with the likelihood of regular "environmental train wrecks," in the words of Secretary of the Interior Bruce Babbitt, to a proactive mode, with measurable benefits to human and natural systems. Hence, freshwater scientists need to develop a predictive capacity that generalizes from experience and replaces the tendency to study each ecosystem and each new stress as if it were unique. Learning (the reduction of uncertainty) now proceeds efficiently among individuals and small research groups. However, the predictive capacity that the nation needs must synthesize experience over long time periods, large spatial scales, and diverse ecosystem types. Learning at these scales will require new institutional structures that provide continuity for long-term studies, mechanisms for collaboration and data sharing among research groups, and opportunities for transdisciplinary synthesis.

Research efforts in predictive management should concentrate on disturbance regimes, physical and biological legacies, integrative ecological properties, modeling (integrating hydrologic, physical, and ecological components and processes), and evaluation (figure 3.7).

Disturbance Regimes   Disturbance regimes are patterns of recurring events, natural or human caused (and the interactions among them), that come from outside a freshwater ecosystem and significantly alter its structure and function. Disturbances such as floods or dewatering, fires, landslides, tree fall, anoxia, changes in land cover or use, and biological invasions and extinctions either act as reset mechanisms for ecosystems or irreversibly alter their structure and function. Research is needed on how changes in frequency, intensity, and duration of disturbance events are influenced by human actions. In addition, we require a predictive understanding of the quantitative effects of disturbances—singly and in combination—at different frequencies, intensities, and durations. One broad question integrates the information needs for disturbance regimes and their effects:

• What disturbance regimes are caused or exacerbated by human activities, and how do they affect the integrity of freshwater ecosystems and the sustainability of water resources?

Physical and Biological Legacies   Legacies are the physical remnants, or "signatures," of past biological and physical disturbances (table 3.1). Legacies have a profound influence on future environmental conditions

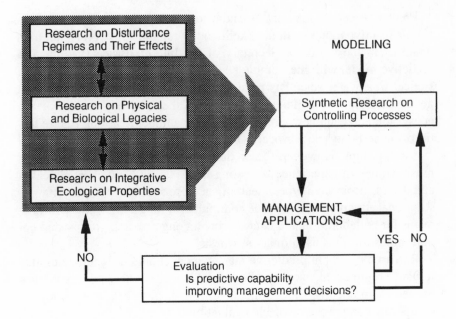

Figure 3.7.   Research Elements in Predictive Management

of ecological systems. In fresh waters, natural legacies comprise the present habitat and biota resulting from past events such as glaciation, floods, sedimentation, and severe anoxia. Past legacies of resource exploitation such as trapping of beaver (*Castor canadensis*), farming practices, timber harvesting, and unregulated mining, have profoundly altered the environmental characteristics of most of the nation's freshwaters, leaving the biophysical legacies that are today's issues. Current anthropogenic activities that produce legacies include habitat alterations as well as conservation practices.

The inherited properties (the physical and biological legacies) of ecological systems determine the directions and rates of ecosystem responses to disturbance or stress. Direction and rate of change are imposed by legacies, and by subsequent disturbances, that are manifested at various times in the future and at various spatial scales. Knowledge of disturbances, legacies, and lag times is crucial to achieving predictive understanding— for example, predicting biodiversity from ecosystem characteristics.

Understanding how past events and processes have led to current legacies or environmental conditions can contribute substantially to predicting the responses of freshwater systems to contemporary disturbances and stresses. Examples of past events are hydrologic modifications (Hunt 1988; Benke 1990), pollutant inputs (Edmondson and Lehman 1981; Nemerow 1991), acid rain and acid deposition (Charles 1991), introduction of exotic species (Moyle 1986; Spencer, McClelland, and Stanford 1991), drought (Hairston and DeStasio 1988), and effects of climate change on freshwater resources (Schindler et al. 1990; Firth and Fisher 1992). Each of these disturbances triggers a cascade of biological and physical effects that become the legacy of the initial disturbance.

Measurable responses of populations, communities, and ecosystems to natural and anthropogenic disturbance and stress (table 3.1) occur over various time scales, depending on the type, intensity, and duration of the disturbance. Some changes occur rapidly, while others are slow, requiring decades or centuries to be completely expressed. Both fast and slow responses to disturbances are difficult to study in the field or to model mathematically. It is known that biotic responses may require multigenerational time scales for communities and populations to express themselves fully (Warner and Chesson 1985; Ellner and Hairston 1994). What is needed for better management is a consideration of how environmental

---

Effects of Hurricanes on Aquatic Consumers

One example of a biological legacy is the significant amount of leaf litter, woody debris, and trees blown into stream channels of the Luquillo Experimental Forest in Puerto Rico during Hurricane Hugo on 18 September 1989. High storm flows associated with the hurricane washed organic debris into large piles along the channel; these debris dams prevented washout of invertebrates and their food supply of decayed leaf litter.

Studies of stream invertebrates (freshwater shrimp) that consume leaf litter were conducted before and after the hurricane (Covich et al. 1991). Three years after the hurricane, populations of freshwater shrimp had doubled in density except in the shallow uppermost pools, where brief tropical storms continued to wash out shrimp in the absence of debris dams.

The hurricane triggered a massive legacy—an input of organic debris that may persist for decades. The initial flood and subsequent storm flows concentrated the debris and thereby increased food availability for shrimp as well as refuge from predators. The initial response of the shrimp population occurred within three years; it is not known how long this response will last or how other components of the ecosystem will respond to the increased density of shrimp in future years.

Table 3.1   Some Examples of Natural and Anthropogenic Disturbances, Legacies, and Effects

Disturbance	Legacies	Effects
Natural		
Tectonic and glacial	*Geomorphic:*	
	Basin morphometry	Influences response to nutrients
	Stream gradient	Influences rates of nutrient spiraling
	Water residence time	Influences response to chemical inputs
Volcanism, fire, and storms	*Biogeochemical:* Bedrock minerals	Determine responses to acid precipitation
	Nutrient release after forest fire	Alters nutrient loading and response times
	Organism transport, dead trees in blowdowns	Provide long-term supply of nutrients
Climate and evolutionary	*Biological:* Postglaciation community composition	Species identity influences ecosystem processes
	Genetic composition	Determines capacity of population and community to respond to environmental change
Anthropogenic		
Forest practices and water management	*Habitat alterations:* Loss of nutrients after deforestation	Decreases long-term supply of nutrients
	Increased water residence time in impoundments	Dictates response to chemical inputs
Urbanization, agricultural development, and water management	*Chemical introductions:* Phosphorus	Release by sediments slows response to sewage diversion; may influence eutrophication
	Toxic organic compounds	Transport and release to groundwater affects biotic communities, even after application is halted
Natural resource management	*Conservation practices:* Biotic community in preserves	Provides a source of organisms for dispersal into and colonization of disturbed areas
	Maintenance of riparian forests	Filters diffuse agriculture inputs
	Maintenance of oxbow lakes	Provides refuge for fish reproduction and development

disturbances create long-term lag times and legacies at the watershed scale. Failure to consider longer temporal and larger spatial scales continues to cause erroneous assessment of environmental relationships and predictions of future conditions. Attention needs to be focused on the following question:

- How do system complexity, uncertainty, and legacy and lag time effects vary in distinct types of freshwater environments?

Integrative Ecological Properties Integrative ecological properties serve as an index of the condition of the human-environmental system. Indicators (such as species richness, trophic composition), ecosystem functions, and biogeochemical states or processes can all serve as integrative ecological properties. Integrative ecological properties (chosen as an index of condition) must be sensitive enough to provide early warning of environmental change as well as be quantitative in order to measure the degree of change that has occurred. Successful predictive management requires that forecasts be made about specific integrative ecological properties through modeling; these properties must then be measured for evaluation of the prediction.

Indicators Any group of biota can indicate environmental condition and change; the research problem is finding appropriate indicators for particular environmental changes. An indicator may be a certain species or group of species or a composite index of a range of community or trophic conditions (Karr 1991). Although the continued presence of a reproducing population indicates that certain environmental conditions exist, the absence of that species does not necessarily indicate unfavorable conditions. The physiology, population biology, and feeding strategies of particular organisms and groups of organisms make them uniquely suited for indicating distinctive aspects of environmental degradation or improvement.

Research is needed to continue to search for and evaluate the significance of biological indicators. For example, the apparent global decline in amphibian species and populations is cause for serious alarm (Wake 1991), but the causes of the decline and the significance of this loss to ecosystems and environmental sustainability are presently unknown. Research addressing the amphibian decline must range in scale from delineation of the physiology of individual organisms to documentation of environmental changes.

Fish, zooplankton, diatoms, and other organisms whose body parts are preserved in sediments provide useful records suggestive of historical changes in trophic structure and chemical conditions. These studies could be expanded in order to improve the use of paleolimnological indicators of natural changes to understand and predict contemporary effects of disturbance at ecosystem and regional scales. Such research would be especially useful in understanding how physical events such as climate change, disturbances, landscape alteration, and change in hydrology generate biotic legacies. For example, diatom species are differentially affected by nutrient concentrations, stoichiometric ratios of chemical elements, and other chemical factors. Diatom populations, which respond quickly to environmental changes because of potentially high growth rates, yield a historical record from the present to thousands of years in the past because diatoms generally are well preserved in lake sediments. Is it possible to link diatom taxa with particular chemical, climate, and trophic regimes to identify indicator species or assemblages as paleolimnological tools for historical climate reconstructions, as has been done for trophic states, pH, and drought?

Finally, there are numerous research opportunities for using cyanobacteria as indicators of change. Research is needed to determine which environmental and genetic conditions activate the toxin-producing processes and what causes these conditions in lakes and wetlands. This research avenue bears directly on the more general issues of activation and inactivation of genes, as with genetically engineered organisms that make their way into the freshwater environment (Tiedje et al. 1989).

Ecosystem Function   Ecosystem functions, such as primary production, decomposition, and food web dynamics, are by definition integrative of terrestrial, atmospheric, and aquatic events occurring within or near the ecosystem. Specific ecosystem functions, combined with selected physical parameters, are strong candidates for tools to measure integrative ecological properties.

Fundamental shifts in ecosystem function indicating that change has occurred should be identified. In addition, a quantitative shift in the process identified would need to be outside the range of natural variability or be a trend away from a normal occurrence. Some combinations of basic ecosystem and physical parameters may be useful in this regard. For instance, a midsummer decrease in mixed-layer depth of lakes that persists over several years would suggest major changes in algal species composition and total primary production. Likewise, optical measurements in water are relatively simple and have the potential to describe ecosystem function in an integrative way. Changes in optical properties of the water would suggest shifts in plankton composition, abundance, and production. Quantification of such measures would prove less costly than overall analysis of several ecosystems or environmental components.

Quantitative methods to describe the food web as an integrative ecosystem function are another major area for research. In addition to traditional labor-intensive methods of measuring growth and consumption by all species in the food web, other approaches may be to utilize organic contaminants (such as DDT) or stable isotopes as food web tracers. Better knowledge of food web dynamics would also contribute to our understanding of such issues as how communities upstream from dams are changed by deletion of migratory fishes, how freshwater ecosystems are changed by modifications to the hydrologic regime, quantitative effects of restoration practices, and cascading effects of fisheries exploitation and hatchery practices on ecosystem characteristics (Carpenter 1988; Spencer et al. 1991; Carpenter and Kitchell 1993; Ludwig, Hilborn, and Walters 1993).

Linking food web dynamics and community succession with watershed management is of high priority for the future. Comparative and experimental studies of inland waters subject to different hydraulic regimes might reveal whether timing or severity of floods could be managed to promote the maintenance of biotic production and community structure over annual to decadal time scales.

Finally, predictive management of chemical contamination should include measurement of chemicals suspected to affect freshwater systems, along with integrative ecological properties. Direct measures and experimentation provide more secure information on cause and effect. However, this task becomes difficult when chemical substances are sequestered among many different biotic and abiotic compartments (for example, algae, fish, and dissolved and particulate materials) or when the technology for detection is elaborate and costly, as for organopesticides. Bioassays will remain an important surrogate for surveillance of chemical inputs and effects. However, short-term bioassays are likely to remain imperfect predictors of longer-term life history and population responses of aquatic organisms (Karr 1993).

Research opportunities addressing contaminants in ecosystems include quantification of the rates and types of transformations introduced chemical substances undergo as they flow through groundwaters and surface waters. What conditions lead to chemical alterations? What are the properties (lability, solubility, toxicity relative to the parent molecule) of the various by-products? Can toxicity and sublethal effects be predicted from molecular structure and environmental conditions? Are some contaminants sufficiently toxic to perturb only certain populations? If so, how taxonomically broad are their effects, and how do aquatic communities respond in the short and long terms? With the nearly eighty thousand human-made chemicals in current use, the several thousand new chemicals manufactured each year, and the enormous nutrient and pesticide additions to the landscape each year, robust indicators of change are imperative.

Biogeochemical Cycles The biogeochemical cycles of major elements such as carbon, oxygen, nitrogen, and sulfur integrate ecological properties and can be used in predictive management. Such an approach does not rely on obtaining data at the species level, as is the case for approaches using indicator organisms and some measure of ecosystem function, such as food web dynamics. Rather, this approach focuses on quantification of the complete cycle or a significant portion of the cycle for single or multiple elements. There is a substantial conceptual base for studying and comparing biogeochemical cycles in aquatic ecosystems. For example, the river continuum concept and the nutrient spiraling concept in stream ecology are both useful for understanding biogeochemical cycling of carbon and nitrogen in streams and rivers (Vannote et al. 1980; Elwood et al. 1983). In addition, these concepts link important biogeochemical cycles in aquatic systems to the larger watershed and to other important physical processes, thus providing an opportunity to gain the broader perspectives necessary for regional-scale issues.

Two research areas should be pursued if studies of biogeochemical cycles are to be useful in a predictive management context. First, information should be collected at a variety of temporal and spatial scales to adequately characterize system variability. For example, research is needed to refine techniques for obtaining detailed data to achieve more precise comparisons over time and among various sites. Second, automated field procedures should be developed for measuring ecosystem functions. For example, measuring photosynthetic rates in streams from diel variations in dissolved oxygen would allow for more frequent and precise measurements and better mathematical analysis of daily variations. Other techniques for measuring rates of biogeochemical transformation, such as carbon dioxide and methane fluxes, could be employed more easily and completely using automated samplers and analyzers. These devices now can be deployed for appropriate time periods at field locations, and remotely obtained data can be transmitted to a central facility. Such approaches are currently being developed in oceanography and environmental engineering for monitoring at remote or hazardous locations and would be useful in evaluating integrative aquatic ecosystem processes resulting from land use changes.

In addition to direct measurements of biogeochemical fluxes, stable isotopes measured in various compartments of an aquatic system can be interpreted in terms of biogeochemical processes. This technique is useful in identifying linkages among adjacent systems (for example, identifying contributions from deep groundwaters to surface waters), in describing the cycling of organic matter, and in evaluating food web structure.

Interpretation of stable isotope data usually involves quantifying ranges of isotopic concentrations, characterizing the composition of source materials, and measuring isotopic fractionations associated with particular processes such as photosynthesis and microbial degradation. Research related to application of isotopic approaches across a range of freshwater ecosystems would be useful in identifying critical ecosystem processes as well as linkages among aquatic ecosystem components. Moreover, because biotic and abiotic compartments can be characterized in the same way, this approach facilitates evaluation of integrated biological, chemical, and hydrologic processes.

Advances in other techniques, such as analysis of trace organic compounds (for example, pigments and lignin degradation products) also can be used to quantify biogeochemical cycles. These techniques are especially useful in paleolimnological interpretation of sediments from lakes and reservoirs. Algal species composition and relative abundance can be determined from residual pigments contained in sediments. Concurrent sediment-dating techniques and pigment analysis can provide a temporal chronology for algal communities identified. Research in this area will benefit our understanding of historical algal communities and their responses to stresses that may have been recorded in sediments, such as previous episodes of contamination.

Finally, there is a need for more in-depth knowledge of biogeochemical cycles over longer periods of time for a range of aquatic systems. Studies in both minimally affected and contaminated or hydrologically stressed environments would be valuable for showing (1) which research and management approaches are most successful for evaluating changes in a particular freshwater system and (2) which types of data are most appropriate for evaluating the modeling results used to predict system-level responses.

Integrated research on controlling processes, drawing from and building on the research described here, can provide the basis for accurate management decisions. However, evaluation will be needed to determine whether the information being generated is adequate for decision makers' needs.

Predictive Modeling   The capacity to make ecological predictions is currently developing in two very different directions. A rich and growing body of comparative models predicts some ecosystem properties from other characteristics (Peters 1986; Cole, Lovett, and Findlay 1991). However, the ability of these models, calibrated across space, to project through time is limited (Pickett 1989). In site-specific studies, time series models can succeed in forecasting dynamics of particular ecosystems (Kitchell 1992; Carpenter and Kitchell 1993). Unfortunately, the extent to which models for one ecosystem can be transferred to other ecosystems is also limited. There is a great need to bring together the two branches of ecological prediction (time and space) to create the capacity to model responses to environmental change for a wide variety of ecosystems and stresses.

Significant advances in predictive modeling include one- and two-dimensional models of temperature and current structure of lakes and estuaries that are now accurate enough to model changes due to varying winds and thermal inputs. For example, DYRESM (the Dynamic Reservoir Simulation Model) has been applied to reservoirs (Imberger and Patterson 1979), freshwater lakes (Patterson, Hamblin, and Imberger 1984), lakes with winter ice cover (Patterson and Hamblin 1988), and salt lakes (Jellison and Melack 1993). Predictive models of this sort can be used to address a variety of environmental problems: assessing dilution of high pollutant loads from incoming streams, determining the effects of high winds on processes at the sediment-water interface, assessing the effects of the El Niño Southern Oscillation on vertical mixing and nutrient supply in stratified lakes, and determining changes in evaporation and thermal structure due to climate warming.

The fluid dynamics of lakes, estuaries, and reservoirs have been resolved well enough in these models to predict thermal structure and oxygen budgets (Patterson, Allanson, and Ivey 1985). The next step is to include ecological processes based on an understanding of the physical mechanisms involved. Coupled physical and biological models are required because biological processes such as photosynthesis depend on vertical mixing for light and nutrient supply. Conversely, physical characteristics such as heat content and thermal structure depend on the concentration of phytoplankton, which is affected by higher trophic levels as well as abiotic factors. Although initial progress in development of models incorporating these interactions has been made (Patterson 1991), further developments require field studies of physical processes as they affect pathways of nutrient supply and distribution of organisms (Statzner, Gore, and Resh 1988).

Solution of Future Problems

Interdisciplinary research programs and investigator-initiated basic research provide outstanding and proven investments toward the nation's capability for detecting and solving unforeseen future problems, the sixth priority research area. Although problem solving involves many aspects, including problem-driven research programs (which can be basic, applied, or a mixture of both), many of our contemporary environmental concerns were first discovered by scientists conducting basic research. For example, the discovery of acid rain in North America was the result of long-term precipitation measurements supporting a study of watershed biogeochemistry (Likens 1992). Similarly, the important role of riparian forests in maintaining environmental quality in streams and rivers was the result of investigations into the fate of fertilizer placed on agricultural fields (Peterjohn and Correll 1984) and studies of the effects of logging (Gregory et al. 1991).

In addition to the discovery of new environmental problems, the knowledge necessary to begin to solve problems often comes from basic research (Edmondson 1991). It has been demonstrated repeatedly that problems are solved most efficiently and completely when a foundation of understanding has been obtained by intensive research. Often, at the time such research is conducted, it is not specifically focused on human-oriented questions. However, there is strong evidence that information obtained from curiosity-driven, investigator-initiated research contributes to an enhanced ability for the United States to manage freshwater resources effectively and at minimal cost. Strengthening of the basic research enterprise is a top priority of the Freshwater Imperative.

Many of the pressing problems resulting from interactions between fresh waters and human society are presently unsolvable. These problems promise to become increasingly complex, contentious, and strategic for the United States with the national and global changes taking place in demographic patterns, resource consumption, environmental vitality, social and institutional organizations, information, and technology (see chapter 2). In a number of areas of limnological study, understanding is inadequate because of simple neglect or because there is only a recent appreciation of an important issue. Physical, biogeochemical, and biological limnology are particularly in need of intensified research (figure 3.8). These specific research areas offer unusual opportunities for rapid and significant scientific advances with particular relevance to emerging human-related problems associated with freshwater resources. In addition, interdisciplinary research and modeling will be needed to couple information gained by fundamental research in all disciplines with new, more comprehensive paradigms. These integrative paradigms will form the basis of a predictive understanding of freshwater systems, which will form the intellectual infrastructure for future needs of policy makers and managers.

Physical Research　Physical limnology has advanced rapidly in the past decade with the stimulus of new instruments, the evaluation of energy budgets within and at the surfaces of lakes, and the infusion of new ideas from oceanography, meteorology, and fluid mechanics (Statzner, Gore, and Resh 1988; Imberger and Patterson 1990). There are new insights into the importance of turbulence and shear stress in structuring and maintaining

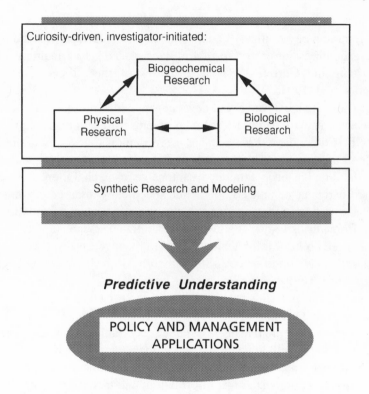

Figure 3.8.   Research Elements in Solution of Future Problems

biological processes as well as new insights into physical processes, other than wind-induced currents, likely to cause movement of materials in lakes. It is now possible to predict upwelling in lakes and to predict whether the upwelling water will originate above or below the thermocline, using dimensionless indices based on a few relatively simple measurements. Likewise, it is now possible to describe flow regimes in streams on microscales relevant to benthic organisms and to describe mechanisms whereby the stream biota enhances rates of resource intake and survival by modifying flow (Dodds 1991; Hart et al. 1991). The success of chemical detection and chemical communication by organisms in different physical flow fields are just two of many exciting advances being made by application of physical research to freshwater systems.

These investigations are proving to be extremely important in understanding the dynamics of freshwater systems and will remain so in the future. However, as the nation looks toward changes that will take place early in the twenty-first century, additional emphasis needs to be given to the following areas:

- Investigations that allow improved predictive understanding over wider spatial and temporal scales. In many cases, the physical processes about which we have new insights have been documented in only a few field situations or laboratory settings. There is a need to verify these processes in a variety of natural systems, determine the time scales on which they occur, quantify their persistence and periodicity, and understand their influences on the biology and chemistry of freshwater ecosystems.

- Research that relates to alteration of natural temperature regimes as well as to water availability for environmental processes. Temperature, a dominant controlling influence on the characteristics of freshwater ecosystems, continues to be altered significantly by global environmental change. What are the implications of temperature change for maintaining the existing characteristics and long-term integrity of the nation's fresh waters? Likewise, as societal demands for fresh water continue to increase, how much fresh water will be needed to maintain the integrity and long-term vitality of freshwater ecosystems and the goods and services they provide?

- An understanding of how the mosaic of biophysical patches and boundaries in watersheds interacts to produce adequate clean water and healthy freshwater environments. As water moves from the atmosphere to land and eventually to the drainage network, it passes through a wide variety of landscape patches and boundaries. These patches and boundaries, with their unique biophysical properties, impart a chemical "signature" on the water, significantly affecting its quality. The enormous changes taking place worldwide in type, size, longevity, and inherent characteristics of patches and boundaries will continue to have profound influences on the supply of fresh water and the vitality of freshwater environments. These pervasive, and probably irreversible, changes make it imperative that scientists and managers develop a predictive understanding of how a watershed's mosaic of patches and boundaries determines water and environmental quality.

Biogeochemical Research Complex interactive chemical and biological transformations occur among compounds as they cycle through freshwater ecosystems. For example, current research is deciphering how organic chemicals bond with metals and how the resulting compounds often become primary sources of carbon and nutrients for microbial metabolism, further mediating the cycling of inorganic nutrients. An understanding of such interactions is essential if freshwater sciences are to provide predictive evaluations of biogeochemical cycling in a changing world. Tracing the sources of materials, their chemical and biological pathways, and their rates of movement through freshwater ecosystems will become more complex with the predicted changes in temperature, hydrology, ultraviolet radiation, concentrations and kinds of chemicals, and shifts in ratios of chemicals.

Temperature and hydrologic regimes exert substantial control on biogeochemical cycles, and research into these factors will continue to produce a better understanding of the processes involved. However, there are several aspects of biogeochemical research that have been neglected but that are suspected to be of immense importance in the near future. These aspects relate to the following:

- Enhanced ultraviolet radiation. Many organic compounds and their biological reactivity are altered through photolysis by ultraviolet radiation. The increase in ultraviolet irradiance caused by reduction of the atmospheric ozone layer has already accelerated decomposition of dissolved organic compounds (Wetzel, Bianchi, and Hatcher 1995) and may be altering rates of microbial metabolism, primary production, and nutrient cycling (Bothwell et al. 1993). The long-term consequences of increased ultraviolet radiation on the integrity of freshwater ecosystems are potentially severe, but little information is available on which to base policy decisions.

- Linked biogeochemical cycles. It is well known that molecules do not cycle independently of other molecules. Linked biogeochemical interactions, particularly among carbon, phosphorus, nitrogen, and sulfur, strongly control the structure and dynamics of freshwater ecosystems. Although considerable progress has been made in understanding cycles of individual molecules in specific freshwater systems, linkages among cycles are poorly known. This is a potentially serious issue for maintaining environmental and socioeconomic integrity with the broad-scale changes taking place in concentrations of molecules, ratios between molecules, introduction of thousands of artificial molecules into the environment, and genetic manipulation of microbes that control rates of chemical cycling. The policy implications of linked biogeochemical cycles will be profound, especially as federal and state governments attempt to implement the Clean Water Act.

- Gas fluxes between fresh waters and the atmosphere. Movement of trace gases between the atmosphere and freshwater ecosystems will become increasingly important as the action of a growing global population continues to increase concentrations of greenhouse gases, particularly carbon dioxide (CO_2) and methane (CH_4). Production of carbon dioxide and methane are especially significant in freshwater ecosystems that have accumulated substantial amounts of organic matter under anaerobic conditions, such as wetlands, shallow lakes, and reservoirs. The role of freshwater ecosystems in affecting climate change probably will be a key issue in the face of continued erosion of soils and organic matter into inland aquatic systems and altered hydrologic regimes that do not allow natural flushing action to occur. An understanding of gas fluxes between fresh waters and the atmosphere also will be of special significance for U.S. environmental policy. As the earth's largest producer of greenhouse gases, it is expected that the United States will face substantial pressure from other nations to reduce gas emissions in the near future. What will be the role of the nation's fresh waters in meeting future international environmental policy goals? This question can be answered only if there is sufficient understanding of biogeochemical controls on gas fluxes and if flux rates of a variety of freshwater environments are known.

Biological Research   The United States has provided international leadership for several decades in understanding the dynamics of freshwater ecosystems and applying this knowledge to resolving many human-caused problems. Notable examples can be found in population and community ecology, ecosystem science, physiological ecology, toxicology, theoretical ecology, fisheries management, and other natural resource sciences. Collectively, the knowledge available from these disciplines and the existing human resources in these areas provide a solid foundation for addressing many emerging issues. The issues are, however, proving increasingly complex as environmental scientists strive for a holistic understanding and policy makers seek resolution of issues at regional to national scales. It is suspected that many emerging biological issues will relate to how organisms respond to environmental change. Consider the following:

- Species persistence and environmental change. A direct consequence of global environmental change will be substantial alterations to the abundance and distribution of freshwater species. An ability to predict changes in species abundance and distribution will require synthesis of existing information on environmental tolerances, the capacity to identify the range of genetic variability inherent within a species, and development of realistic scenarios about future changes in habitat. This also includes information on the mobility of native organisms needed for recolonization of restored water bodies relative to the mobility of invasive exotic species. Collectively, this knowledge will be needed to make predictions about the ability of species to persist under new combinations of environmental conditions. In addition, knowledge is needed regarding the environmental effects of losses of particular species and the consequences for environmental stability of reduced species diversity.

- Theory development. Historically, much of the basis for management of our nation's fresh waters and for education of several generations of resource managers has been related to theoretical models developed more than forty years ago (such as the logistic, Lotka-Volterra, and density-dependent stock recruitment models in fisheries). Despite considerable attention to these theoretical models in the scientific and managerial literature, it is clear that they are often oversimplifications based on faulty biological assumptions (Walters 1986; Botkin 1990). Recently, on reexamination of considerable data, it has been discovered that none of them supports the original predictions (Hall 1988). The implications for effective long-term management of our nation's freshwater resources are severe, underscoring the urgent need to develop valid natural resource models that are adaptable to unforeseen conditions. A predictive understanding of fundamental factors affecting aquatic production, controls on ecosystem properties, and long-term vitality of aquatic systems will require new approaches to modeling (and model validation) that are immensely more sophisticated than those currently in use (Carpenter 1988; Carpenter and Kitchell 1993). In addition, development of theoretical models of genealogical relationships of taxa are needed to predict yet-unobserved characteristics and environmental constraints for taxa.

- Sensitive landscape components. As cultivation and civilization expand, concomitant changes occur in the mosaic of landscape patches and characteristics of the boundaries between the patches. Communities at the boundaries between terrestrial and freshwater ecosystems are particularly sensitive to landscape change (Naiman and Décamps 1990). Examples include riparian forests, marginal wetlands, littoral lake zones, floodplain lakes and forests, and areas with significant groundwater–surface water exchange. These areas are rich in natural resources, biological diversity, and habitat for threatened species. They are also important in controlling the movement of nutrients and other materials from land to water and in influencing local climate conditions. Alarmingly, anthropogenic changes in boundaries between land and water are proceeding without sufficient information on their environmental implications. An emerging issue is whether human-created boundaries will have the same properties as natural boundaries.

These physical, biogeochemical, and biological issues are only a few examples of the tasks awaiting the nation's freshwater scientists and managers in the near future. Additional future issues can only be imagined as new chemicals are introduced, as societal values and attitudes change, as demographic patterns shift to an older and more urbanized society, and as consumption and technology adjust to form the future nation. Collectively, these changes, and the essential nature of fresh water to the nation's character and socioeconomic strength, argue strongly for a substantially improved scientific and managerial infrastructure—the basis for a thoughtful national and international environmental policy.

4

Linking Research, Management, and Policy

Effective integration of the Freshwater Imperative research agenda with management and policy is essential to achieve new perspectives as well as new interdisciplinary approaches to freshwater problems in the United States. Proactive and continuous interaction between limnological researchers and the personnel responsible for fulfilling various government management mandates is vital to development and implementation of a progressive national water policy that can meet the challenges presented in chapter 3. This chapter proposes specific linkages between the FWI research agenda and water resources management—both of which are influenced by local, state, regional, and national water policies. Although the following recommendations focus on government management, it is implicit that development of a progressive water resource policy must also include private landowners and nongovernmental organizations (NGOs). It is expected that inclusion of these groups will be coordinated by the appropriate government agencies as the nation develops a strengthened philosophy of stewardship and responsibility toward freshwater resources. In addition, the relationship between science, management, and policy requires mechanisms for regular assessment to continually strengthen the connections. Given the urgency and scale of freshwater issues, especially conservation and rehabilitation, it is evident that many management and policy decisions must be made soon and without a predictive understanding of freshwater systems.

Interfaces Between Natural, Human, and Management Sciences

Freshwater ecosystems provide strategic resources vital to human societies (table 4.1). In many respects, the well-being of individuals, communities, and nations is determined by availability of freshwater and the ecological and social goods and services provided by freshwater ecosystems. In obtaining these benefits, we divert nearly 5,000 cubic kilometers (1,300 trillion gallons) of water worldwide from natural ecosystems for all human uses each year (Engelman and LeRoy 1993; National Research Council 1991). The net result is that the natural characteristics and products of fresh water have been widely disrupted, creating an urgent need for effective management and policy.

Demand for fresh water and aquatic ecological goods and services increases as the nation's population increases. Yet the freshwater supply is finite. Supply varies from year to year and from place to place in association with climate, but on the average about 2,480 cubic kilometers (660 trillion gallons) of freshwater is all the United States has available each year to maintain freshwater ecosystems and to provide beneficial uses for the nation's growing population. Moreover, the self-renewal capacity of freshwater ecosystems to produce goods and services is too often compromised by the destructive ways in which those benefits are realized. In most large watersheds throughout the world, self-renewal capacity is degraded in proportion to the number of people living within the watershed (McDonnell and Pickett 1993). A vicious circle exists: Freshwater supply is finite in relation to environmental needs, the human population, and the hydrologic cycle. The usefulness of water to human social systems (that is, water quality) is determined by the vitality and recycling efficiency of freshwater ecosystems. Yet the ever-increasing number of humans continually compromises this self-renewal capacity through cumulative effects imposed by a growing demand for water.

Hence a plethora of federal, state, and local statutes regulate use of fresh water through the principles of conservation and fairness. Moreover, the commodity value of fresh water increases as supply dwindles, fostering construction of more sophisticated water regulation structures and delivery systems. In developed countries, mitigation of negative effects associated with water development activities often includes human-engineered systems such as sewage treatment systems and commercial fish hatcheries. Yet human-engineered systems are too often ineffectual, very costly, or both. To protect and conserve freshwater ecosystems there is an urgent need to better understand the complex linkages between natural and human elements of the ecosystems; thereby decreasing dependence on human-engineered systems. Indeed, the FWI emphasizes that freshwater ecosystems must be examined in the context of (1) natural biophysical attributes and processes (natural sciences), (2) innate human tendencies that influence demographics, such as culture, history, and eco-

Table 4.1   Some Benefits Humans Derive from Freshwater Ecosystems

Direct Use of Surface Waters and Groundwaters
Preparation and cooking of household and commercial food products
Drinking, personal hygiene, waste disposal, other household cleaning tasks
Agricultural irrigation
Water for livestock, poultry production
Power generation:
  Hydropower
  Temperature regulation and heat transfer in other power-producing processes
    (geothermal, nuclear, coal, etc.)
  Peak load power management in pumped storage systems
Energy transfer in heating and cooling applications
Manufacturing uses
Fire fighting

Products Harvested from Healthy Freshwater Ecosystems
Fish and wildlife (commercial and subsistence harvest)
Riparian forest products (e.g., timber, mushrooms)
Vegetable products from wetlands, bogs, and lakes (e.g., rice, peat, cranberries)
Streambed minerals and materials (e.g., gravel, sand)

Services Provided by Healthy Freshwater Ecosystems
Recreation (sportfishing, hunting, boating, swimming)
Transportation of goods
Freshwater storage (in glaciers, watersheds)
Flood control
Nutrient deposition in floodplain agricultural areas
Natural purification of human wastes
Habitat for biological diversity
Moderation and stabilization of urban and natural microclimates
Moderation of global climate (e.g., "greenhouse effect," reflection of solar radiation from snow)
Nutrient balancing and buffering of rivers (reduction of red tides, etc.)
Aesthetics and mental health

nomics (human sciences), and (3) government policies and statutes (management science).

Another key premise of the FWI research agenda is that there must be an interactive relationship between basic research and management and policy processes and that this relationship must take place over both short and long time frames and in terms easily understood by the public. Managers must respond to the need for investment in basic research, and researchers must be cognizant of information needs of managers. Basic research in limnology too often requires years to be effectively translated and utilized by managers (figure 4.1). The links between research and management need to be effective and respectful. To deal with the pervasive problems regarding water supply and habitat, the FWI recommends a new approach that builds a solid foundation of knowledge about the structure, function, and dynamics of freshwater ecosystems so that socioeconomic and political processes influencing water policies can interact with a fully informed management process (figure 4.2). The cohesive element in this new approach is effective information transfer between the scientific and managerial disciplines involved in understanding and regulating regional freshwater ecosystems.

In the model shown in figure 4.3, the natural sciences referred to are integrative sciences such as limnology, ecology, and hydrology as well as disciplines such as geology, botany, zoology, chemistry, and physics, all of which provide an understanding of some aspect of the natural world. Collectively, the human sciences describe and explain the behavior of human populations and are represented by economics, geography, sociology, political science, and law. Management sciences include restoration ecology, conservation biology, fisheries management, forestry, resource policy and management, and water resource and environmental engineering. The value of the conceptual framework presented in figure 4.3 is that it defines the role of limnologists in building a better understanding of freshwater systems, developing new technologies, and addressing future freshwater

Traditional Approach to Freshwater Research and Management

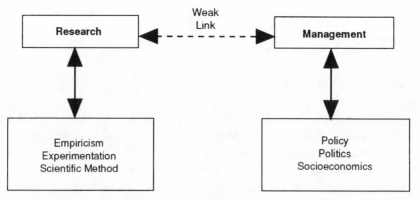

Figure 4.1   Information Transfer Between Research and Management. This link has traditionally been weak because of differing foundations and lack of interactions at all levels (Adapted from Stanford and Ward 1992b).

issues. Moreover, the conceptual framework establishes pathways for information transfer among the sciences that provide the foundation for effective water policy.

Linking the sciences involved in water research and management can be accomplished by viewing water problems holistically and integrating research and management into a regional ecosystem context (figure 4.2; see also Naiman 1992). Of equal importance is transmitting scientific information to national leaders and the public in a manner that will produce an informed and responsive citizenry that is willing and able to provide direct feedback to scientific programs. This may be approached in two ways. First, freshwater scientists must become visible and influential at the community level in an active but advisory manner. The role of freshwater scientists should be to examine and explain the scientific implications of national policies and local, state, and national statutes. Second, the scientific community must be involved (as advisors) in political processes,

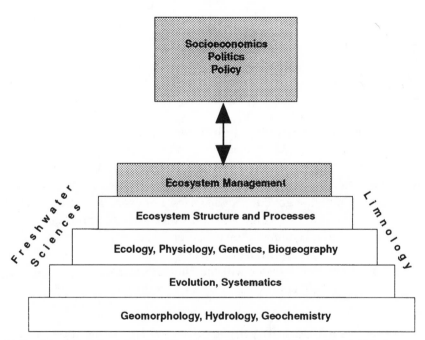

Figure 4.2 A New Perspective for Freshwater Research and Management. This new perspective involves policies and management actions (shaded) that are founded on sound limnological science derived from basic research (nonshaded) (Adapted from Stanford and Ward 1992b).

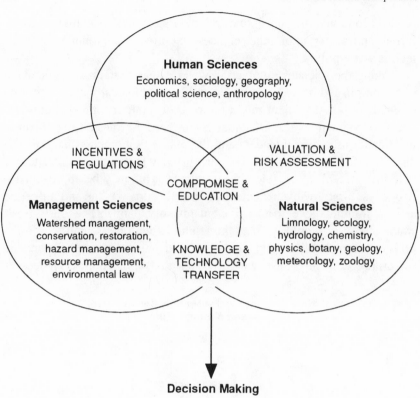

Decision Making

Figure 4.3   Interfaces of Human, Natural, and Management Sciences (Adapted from Orians et al. 1990.)

such as reauthorization of the Clean Water and Endangered Species Act. This involvement would help ensure that policies and statutes are consistent with current science (see figure 4.3). and it can be accomplished by scientific societies investing in information networks with Congress, state legislatures, and other government agencies. For example, the Ecological Society of America's Washington, D.C., office assists in making ecological issue papers and comments on behalf of the society available to members of Congress and government agencies and their staffs. Only through effective information transfer will the United States develop a national water policy that will conserve and enhance freshwater resources.

Key Issues Influencing Integration of the Sciences

The FWI research agenda proposes a research base for development of policies that protect, restore, and enhance the nation's freshwater resources.

Although much of the work can be done by research universities and research units within federal agencies, such as the National Biological Service, many ongoing scientific programs in the United States involve activities that relate to particular management mandates. For example, the Forest Service is required to minimize the influence of logging on water quality and habitat and therefore must evaluate logging impacts and apply management practices to minimize such impacts. Evaluation of impacts and development of new management approaches (applied research) currently consumes a large percentage of the agencies' annual research budgets. Innovative administrative approaches to integrating management and science, such as combining socioeconomic, environmental, and managerial scientists on a team to design, conduct, and analyze the research, could provide large dividends for the nation's fresh waters.

The conceptual framework for linking human, natural, and management sciences presented in figure 4.3 implies that applied research by the management sciences must be complementary to more basic research by the natural and human sciences. Indeed, effective resource management is a formalized process that involves several specific steps: (1) prediction of environmental end points associated with a suite of management actions designed to confront an uncertainty, such as the effect of different logging protocols on fine sediments in streams; (2) implementation of the most ecologically and economically rational actions; (3) monitoring and evaluation of management actions; and (4) a shift to alternative actions as indicated by monitoring and evaluation. Known as adaptive management (Lee 1993), this stepwise procedure, when implemented correctly, integrates results of basic research into the management process and provides a context for applied research that will strengthen predictive management (step 1). However, the management process will always be framed by policy; for example, minimizing stream sedimentation may not be possible if policy requires removing trees from the watershed. Moreover, management processes may be completely compromised by conflicting mandates, such as extracting resources while completely protecting water quality or habitat.

Recognizing current opportunities to redirect agency funds, the following model was developed for identifying and prioritizing research that will stimulate effective linkages between research, management, and policy. In this model, research priorities can be derived in the context of improving management, and policy. Model guidelines relate to existing level of knowledge, extent of degradation, ability to extrapolate results, credibility of protocols, and the protocols' importance to relevant policy issues (table 4.2).

Table 4.2   Attributes of New Research Needed for
Proactive Management and Policy Development

---

1. The information and understanding to be derived from the research will influence policies and regulations that prevent degradation of freshwater ecosystems

2. The extent of the degradation to be ameliorated is significant and widespread, with the strong likelihood that the research will yield information to alter policy or produce regulatory changes

3. The information and understanding to be produced by new research cannot be extrapolated or synthesized with confidence from existing research results

4. The results of the research, when used to change policy, will have clear potential for positive influence to protect or restore freshwater ecosystems

5. The research must be technically and scientifically sound

6. Linkage between research results and government use in policy analysis must be demonstrable

---

Three general areas of applied research should be pursued by interactive, multidisciplinary approaches at a regional ecosystem level: (1) evaluating best management practices with respect to land and water use, (2) applying new types of ecological engineering and planning to mitigate degradation of water and aquatic habitats by human use, and (3) providing regional approaches to monitoring and assessment to stimulate integration of aquatic resource management efforts (and thereby reduce conflict between policy and management objectives). These general subjects fit the adaptive management concept with respect to understanding, conserving, and enhancing freshwater ecosystems.

Critical Evaluation of Best Management Practices

Best management practices (BMPs), a term generally taken to mean state-of-the-art environmental protection measures, have both succeeded and failed to (1) ameliorate adverse cumulative effects, (2) protect natural interactions between fresh water and the land, and (3) preserve the integrity of aquatic communities (Bisson et al. 1992). Yet in many regions, BMPs associated with industrialization, urbanization, farming, ranching, timber harvesting, and mining are the dominant causes of degradation of freshwater ecosystems. Many of these activities are already managed through regulations and incentives. The key challenge is to quantitatively link these controls on human actions to direct and indirect consequences for freshwater resources. The objective is twofold: (1) to limit negative influences on freshwater ecosystems through improved land and water

Adaptive Management of Large Ecosystems

As Kai Lee commented in his book *Compass and Gyroscope,* "One of the peculiar commonplaces of our time is the realization that civilized life cannot continue in its present form" (Lee 1993). With Columbia River salmon as a case study, Lee laid out an approach to achieving a sustainable future through adaptive management and bounded conflict resolution. The Columbia River is the fourth largest river in North America; as with other large ecosystems such as the Great Lakes and the Everglades, its resources and problems involve a number of regional governments and conflicting uses. For example, when hydropower dams were constructed along the Columbia River, intense development of the region followed, accompanied by significant environmental costs. Predevelopment salmon populations approximated 11 million adults annually for the Columbia River, of which 77 percent used the upper river for spawning. In the late 1970's and early 1980's, however, spawning runs averaged only 3 million per year, with only 42 percent using the waters above Bonneville Dam. Today, two-thirds of Columbia River salmonids come from hatcheries. This decline in salmon not only represents depleted resources; to many it has degraded the very spirit of the Pacific Northwest. The salmonid resource has become more dependent on hatcheries, and use of hatchery production has contributed further to the decline of natural stocks. Additional stresses on the Columbia River ecosystem include fishing and agriculture use of water.

In moving toward a sustainable future, human interaction with such complex real-world problems can best be guided by adaptive management (Lee's "compass") and bounded conflict (his "gyroscope"). "*Adaptive management* is an approach to natural resource policy that embodies a simple imperative: policies are experiments; *learn from them.*" In order to live, humans must use aquatic resources, but, Lee says, we "do not understand nature well enough to know how to live harmoniously within environmental limits. Adaptive management takes that uncertainty seriously, treating interventions in natural systems as experimental probes." More sharply honed than simple trial-and-error learning, this approach plans for unanticipated outcomes by collecting and evaluating information. Results from adaptive management reduce uncertainty in the expected outcomes of human interaction with nature.

Adaptive management is a key to learning efficiently from human interaction with large aquatic ecosystems. This approach integrates management and acquisition of new knowledge in the longer time frames and larger spatial scales needed as the nation grapples with complex problems involving the use and rehabilitation of aquatic ecosystems.

stewardship and (2) to provide scientific evaluation to policy makers so that failing practices can be eliminated or changed by public mandate. With careful planning, evaluation can be conducted concurrently with land and water resources management. For example, a proper experimental design to evaluate different logging procedures on stream sediment loading can be evaluated within the framework of removing timber for economic reasons.

Using an Ecological Approach in Environmental Engineering

Water resource development in the United States has been extensive, involving construction of dams, locks, and diversions for irrigation and water conveyance channels. Water resource development and operational practices are aimed at controlling water quantity, storing water through drought periods, preventing floods, transferring water to cities or irrigable cropland, providing commercial navigation, and generating hydropower. These engineered systems are generally optimized solely for the purposes for which they were created, but it is now necessary to optimize their with respect to conservation and enhancement of freshwater ecosystems in addition to their historical goals. The amount of uniformity manifest in the massive water engineering projects in the United States strongly suggests that these systems could be operated in more creative ways to enhance freshwater systems. For example, a large body of scientific information has shown that productive commercial and sport fisheries can exist downstream from large reservoirs provided dam operations optimize flow and temperature conditions in tailwaters (Ward and Stanford 1979, 1991; Lillehammer and Saltveit 1984; Craig and Kemper 1987).

Complex models for water resource management are now used to consider hydrologic processes such as precipitation, runoff, and evapotranspiration as well as natural variation in precipitation and climate while optimizing water storage and hydropower (National Research Council 1991). The challenge for the future will be to design, construct, and operate civil works in ways that also sustain the long-term ecological integrity of freshwater ecosystems. Of particular importance are long-term effects of water projects on the amount and routing of water and waterborne materials along the flow path to the ocean as well as maintenance of sufficient habitat for the persistence of species with their natural genetic variability.

Monitoring and Assessment

An important function of freshwater ecosystems is the support of living aquatic resources, including sport and commercial fisheries, wild rice, molluscs, and crayfish. In many regions, these living resources

Lakes as Indicators of National Water Quality

More than 80 percent of the nation's population lives within 8 km (5 miles) of surface waters. Hence, surface water characteristics are sensitive integrators of land use activities. Lakes, for example, are natural ledgers that tell the story of humankind's environmental accountability or lack thereof. For instance, lake sediments provide an accurate record of what the nation has done to the environment. Lakes are benchmarks for demonstrating how to maintain water quality and rehabilitate ecosystems (Edmondson 1991, 1994), provided there is an investment in long-term analyses documenting limnological conditions so that change over time can be quantified.

Unfortunately, there are only a few accurate, long-term (more than ten years) data sets describing limnological conditions for lakes nationwide. Even for the Laurentian Great Lakes, which are of critical economic importance to our nation, trends in water quality are poorly demonstrated because of overlapping jurisdictions and lack of continuity and quality control in data gathering. Notable examples of lakes for which accurate, long-term data do exist include Lake Washington in Washington State (Edmondson 1991), Flathead Lake in Montana (Stanford and Ward 1992b), Lake Tahoe in California and Nevada (Goldman 1993), and Lake Mendota in Wisconsin (Kitchell 1992).

Relationship between Algal Growth and Human Population Growth

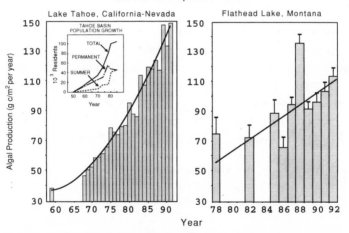

Long-term studies at Lake Tahoe (left) and Flathead Lake (right), two of our nation's largest and most pristine lakes, show that chronic deterioration of water quality (defined by increasing growth of algae) is directly related to increasing human activities within the lakes' watersheds (data from Goldman 1993 and Stanford et al. 1992). Controlling the effects of eutrophication will require a continuing effort not only to restrict the sources of nutrients but also to widen the search for alternative approaches. These alternative approaches will require application of existing knowledge regarding factors controlling rates of primary production and the structure of phytoplankton communities as well as continued generation of new knowledge.

have diminished over the past two decades (see chapter 2). Aspects of the research program described in chapter 3, such as the elements discussed under modified hydrologic flow patterns and maintenance of biodiversity, will improve understanding of these declines. However, sustaining of aquatic resources will also require better ecological monitoring and assessment with respect to environmental change. Indeed, it has been argued that the effectiveness of the Federal Clean Water Act and Endangered Species Act cannot be accurately evaluated because adequate nationwide monitoring and assessment are lacking.

Water quality monitoring by the U.S. Geological Survey (the NASQAN and NAWQA programs) and the U.S. Environmental Protection Agency (EMAP program) (Britton, Goddard, and Briggs 1983; Hirsch, Alley, and Wilber 1988; Thorton, Hyatt, and Chapman 1993; Gurtz 1994) employs a diffuse network of sites that may serve in the resolution of some issues if carefully linked to research objectives such as those described in chapter 3. Most U.S. government monitoring programs do not operate within an ecosystem context that recognizes large lakes, wetlands, or rivers as integrators of the cumulative effects of human activities; nor, in most cases, are they able to identify specific causes for environmental trends.

Management agencies tend to focus monitoring and assessment on single attributes of freshwater ecosystems. Often those attributes do not integrate the ecosystem. The result is "interference management," in which actions designed to enhance one ecological attribute result in unanticipated negative effects on others (Stanford and Ward 1992a). These "management train wrecks" could be greatly reduced or avoided through a broader scientific synthesis of available information and effective use of adaptive management concepts (Walters 1986; Lee 1993). Unfortunately, due to a lack of comprehensive evaluation and synthesis, many freshwater issues are overly controversial.

Institutional Mechanisms to Link Research and Management

A basic tenet of the FWI is that activities and expertise at traditional research institutions need to be coordinated with agencies and other entities that manage freshwater ecosystems and their catchments. Interdisciplinary, collaborative research efforts within traditional research institutions are needed to examine the structure and function of freshwater ecosystems in the context of the issues described herein. At the same time, management agencies need to initiate or expand collaborative activities with research institutions. Traditionally, management agencies have contracted with research institutions for specific studies. Although this should continue, additional interactive routine discussions of research priorities for management science are needed based on syntheses of human and natural sciences. In short, research needs to be responsive to the needs of management but not driven by management objectives.

Federal agencies with organized research units in place do not necessarily offer effective models for linking research and management (for example, the U.S. Geological Survey and the National Park Service). Although local consortia exist in some areas, these agreements are either limited or, in some cases, legislated by state government. Hence, federal and private participation in broad-based consortia is not necessarily binding.

The recent reorganization of Department of the Interior research personnel into the National Biological Service (NBS) may offer an opportunity to create an innovative model that would also be used by other government agencies. The NBS is envisioned as a mechanism to link the research and management mandates of the Department of the Interior and advise other federal departments, such as the USDA Forest Service. Fulfilling this mandate will require cooperative research within several ecoregions or regional ecosystems (Raven et al. 1993). Major universities and research institutions in each ecoregion could serve as interdisciplinary bases of operation for regional NBS offices to foster linkages between the research and management communities. The existing cooperative park study units and cooperative fish and wildlife units have functioned in this way for many years. However, they have never had sufficient budgets to accomplish regional ecosystem synthesis. The FWI envisions a seven-step implementation procedure:

1. National Biological Service offices are established at major universities within ecoregions or states, recognizing the need for NBS scientists to work closely with scientists from universities and private industry. Qualified NBS scientists are given faculty status, and university scientists are involved in NBS programs.

2. Through liaison with local management personnel (forest supervisors, state lands specialists, park superintendents) and governments (states, tribes, counties) and using the FWI research agenda as a guide, the regional NBS office identifies freshwater issues that require research and that are consistent with national policies.

3. Each NBS office develops hypothesis-based research proposals that are responsive to identified freshwater research issues. In most cases, long-term (five years or more) approaches are utilized. All or most of the proposals involve scientists from a broad array of research institutions and scientific disciplines. Cooperative research can be partially financed by reducing duplication of expertise and facilities already extant at research institutions.

4. A formal merit review process patterned after that of the National Science Foundation is used to prioritize and fund research projects. A budget for the review process is established, including remuneration to reviewers.

5. Research is conducted based on an annual budget process for each state or ecoregion under the auspices of the national NBS office.

6. Research performance is determined in the form of peer-reviewed articles in professional journals and books. Technical report writing is minimized. Moreover, evaluations of NBS scientists are based on the performance standards of publication and public service that currently define scientific excellence.

7. Meetings and conferences within a region are held annually to assist the transfer of new information to managers and to allow the research community to receive suggestions about management problems that require data, synthesis, or new research. Information transfer also occurs at meetings of professional societies by requiring participation by NBS scientists as a part of their annual performance evaluation.

The FWI strategy is a radical departure from the status quo. Other concepts may improve on the one proposed here. However, the FWI strongly emphasizes the need for integration of sciences and institutions with respect to developing a predictive understanding of freshwater ecosystems so that our nation's aquatic resources may be understood, conserved, and enhanced for human benefit.

5

Implementation Requirements

Implementation of the priority research efforts identified by the Freshwater Imperative involves changes in institutions as well as improvements in infrastructure (figure 5.1). The actions suggested in this book will demand administrative leadership and vision. Yet these actions will ensure that an adequate base of information and expertise is available as the nation faces water-related threats to its quality of life and the sustainability of the environment and human culture.

The scope of most water-related environmental issues exceeds the capacity of individual institutions or nations to resolve them. Coordination of efforts across governments, agencies, academia, and the private sector is vital for comprehensive coverage of the issues and intelligent use of scarce resources.

Implementation of the FWI research agenda as described in chapters 3 and 4 will require creative leveraging of existing funds as well as requests for new funds. It is estimated that the annual cost of the FWI will be less than 1 percent of what the United States spends annually on regulatory and remedial protection of its waters. Given the need to respond to these human and environmental challenges in an appropriate and timely fashion, it is the considered professional opinion of the FWI Steering Committee and the professional societies supporting the FWI that the research agenda is thoroughly justified. The FWI's perspective is that the proposed research and associated expenditures of U.S. government funds will become an integral part of regulation and remedial protection of United States waters. The proposed research will (1) build a better scientific understanding of freshwater systems for the future and (2) address current research needs related to the specific missions of government agencies in a coordinated and efficient manner.

As freshwater science scales up to a regional, longer-term focus, several general recommendations may be made for maintaining and enhancing the intellectual and technical vigor of the discipline. These include ensuring continuance of long-term studies; including social and economic models

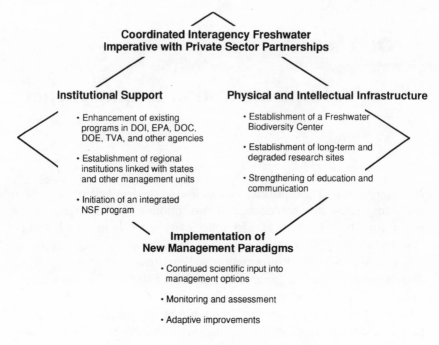

Coordinated Interagency Freshwater Imperative with Private Sector Partnerships

Institutional Support

• Enhancement of existing programs in DOI, EPA, DOC, DOE, TVA, and other agencies

• Establishment of regional institutions linked with states and other management units

• Initiation of an integrated NSF program

Physical and Intellectual Infrastructure

• Establishment of a Freshwater Biodiversity Center

• Establishment of long-term and degraded research sites

• Strengthening of education and communication

Implementation of New Management Paradigms

• Continued scientific input into management options

• Monitoring and assessment

• Adaptive improvements

Figure 5.1   Implementation Recommendations

in ecological studies; augmenting data acquisition at long-term monitoring sites to include experimental and modeling components; organizing efforts to coordinate with sites outside the United States to produce a global perspective; expanding the applicability of general ecological principles; and coordinating efforts with the Center for Environmental Analysis and Synthesis (a newly-formed collaborative research center focusing on major fundmental and applied problems facing ecology) for enhanced synthesis of data, models, and concepts derived from regional sites.

The Strategic Centerpiece

The centerpiece of the recommended FWI implementation strategy is a coordinated, interagency initiative with private sector partnerships (figure 5.2). This Freshwater Imperative would be expected to mature into a freshwater research program drawing on the expertise of agency scientists and managers, academic researchers, and private sector groups. It would focus efforts on the key freshwater issues of aquatic ecosystem integrity and human health and safety, especially as related to water availability

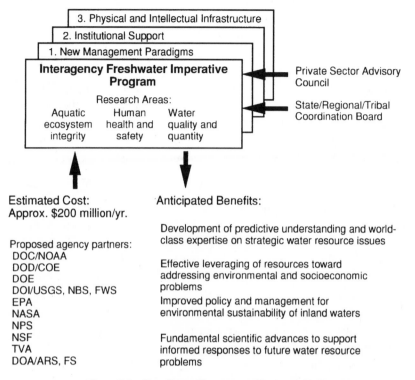

Figure 5.2   Coordinated Interagency Budget Initiative

(quality, quantity, and timing). This focus can be obtained through the specific research elements detailed in chapters 3 and 4.

The Freshwater Imperative research program should be patterned, at least in part, on successful interagency efforts such as the U.S. Global Change Research Program and the U.S. Weather Research Program. It also should be planned to ensure proper balance among physical, ecological, and social dimensions of the scientific problems. The Freshwater Imperative should not attempt to duplicate successful ongoing activities but rather should provide a framework for coordination and a strategy for coupling efforts among agencies and between the federal government and nonfederal partners. The emphasis should be on better coordination, better connections among scientists and decision makers, and strong support for issue-focused research. An integrated advisory council of private sector and state, regional, and tribal scientists and managers should convene regularly to guide the program and ensure that coordination with these partners is effective.

Agencies that have expressed interest in the Freshwater Imperative to date include the Environmental Protection Agency, the Department of the

Interior, the National Science Foundation, the Department of Energy, the Department of Commerce, the Tennessee Valley Authority, the National Aeronautics and Space Administration, the Department of Defense, and the Department of Agriculture. Others are expected to become interested as the program develops further. A coordinated research program will help address the problem of division in agency mandates. A number of agencies have responsibility for and authority over water resource issues with little incentive to cooperate. Often the agencies' missions cause them to be diametrically opposed, making the Department of Justice the de facto natural resource manager. Collaborative research efforts should encourage cooperation among federal agencies and among federal, state, local, and tribal agencies and universities on public and private lands.

Private sector partners might include the types of participants that were involved in Water Quality 2000: representatives of agricultural and industrial constituencies, conservation and environmental nongovernmental organizations (NGOs), private landowners with large holdings, the academic community, the recreational sector, and the environmental consulting community. A coordinated program with these groups should foster the development of powerful partnerships between university and private sector scientists and managers and their federal counterparts. This strategy directly supports current federal efforts to forge a closer working partnership among industry, federal and state government agencies, and universities.

Agencies with responsibility for freshwater research and development should coordinate roles, responsibilities, and budgets of science projects, and agency plans should consider intramural and extramural research allocations for directed programs and for investigator-initiated research. The implementation recommendations presented in figure 5.1 provide several tangible examples of potential interagency coordinated efforts. For example, the Freshwater Biodiversity Center and regional institutions could be jointly supported by several agencies to meet their specific missions. Currently, the DOI and the EPA need taxonomic information on freshwater organisms and maintenance of reference collections. These needs could be partially met by the Freshwater Biodiversity Center, which also could support investigator-initiated research on freshwater biodiversity with funding from the NSF, the DOI, and the EPA. Concomitantly, regional institutions should involve the cooperative units, district offices, and regional offices of such agencies as the U.S. Fish and Wildlife Service (FWS), the USDA Forest Service (FS), the EPA, and the U.S. Geological Survey (USGS), with research and educational efforts supported by the cooperating agencies.

One model for the administration and management of these FWI research centers is through a consortium of federal and state agencies and academic institutions. Large research centers, such as the National Center for Atmospheric Research, are currently managed through a consortium of academic institutions; an expansion of this approach may be successful in implementing the FWI research agenda.

The FWI program also will help bring together the many relevant scientific disciplines, which too often operate separately from one another. As stated throughout this book, both disciplinary and interdisciplinary approaches to research are necessary to resolve the most significant questions currently facing the nation. A coordinated research program will ensure that adequate attention is given to development of fundamental knowledge underpinning management and policy decisions. A gap now exists in the federal science structure charged with generating this knowledge—an especially alarming situation given the pressure to direct science spending toward technological innovation with international trade and business potential.

The Freshwater Imperative should be continually refined as new knowledge becomes available and as emerging freshwater issues demand responses. As the FWI matures into a research program, it will require sustained effort to maintain vision and to be accountable.

Estimated Cost

The Freshwater Imperative research program is expected to cost approximately $200 million per year (in fiscal year 1994 dollars) for focused programs, including bolstering the research component for some ongoing activities, such as monitoring and assessment programs of the EPA and the DOI and management activities of the TVA and the FS (table 5.1). Focused programs on ecological restoration, maintenance of biodiversity, modified hydrologic regimes, ecosystem goods and services, predictive management, and solution of future problems should all be part of this activity.

Contributory programs—those that contribute to the objectives of the program but whose main focus may differ—will probably represent a similar amount. These programs might include, for example, socioeconomic assessments, policy analyses, and technology transfer programs.

Anticipated Benefits

The Freshwater Imperative will move the United States toward development of predictive understanding and world-class expertise on strategic issues of both local importance and global significance. The proposed program will encourage more effective leveraging of scarce fiscal resources

Table 5.1   Projected Annual Costs for Implementation
of the Freshwater Imperative

Component of Program	Cost (millions of dollars per year)
New Management Paradigms	**20**
Institutional Support	
Enhancement of existing programs	60
Establishment of regional institutions	60
Initiation of new NSF program	10
Total institutional support	**130**
Physical and Intellectual Research Infrastructure	
Establishment of Freshwater Biodiversity Center	15
Establishment of long-term and degraded research sites	20
Strengthening of education and communication	15
Total research infrastructure	**50**
Total costs	**200**

toward addressing environmental and socioeconomic problems. It will
also improve policy and management decision making directed toward the
environmental sustainability of inland waters. Finally, the Freshwater Imperative will promote fundamental advances in knowledge to support informed responses to future problems.

New Management Paradigms

The importance of integrating science and decision making is emphasized
by the implementation of new management paradigms (figure 5.3; see also
chapter 4). Many agencies are already moving toward an ecosystem management approach to their missions. The Freshwater Imperative supports
this movement and encourages incorporation of an integrated watershed
management perspective into programs and projects. Key elements of this
approach are a science-management-policy partnership, increased resources for extramural research, and freshwater scientific advisory panels
to make recommendations to heads of agencies.

The integrated watershed management approach as described by Gene
Likens (1992) depends on an agreement by scientists to work with managers to formulate and help answer questions while making clear the existing level of uncertainty and additional research that needs to be done. It
must be backed by an agreement by managers to give serious considera-

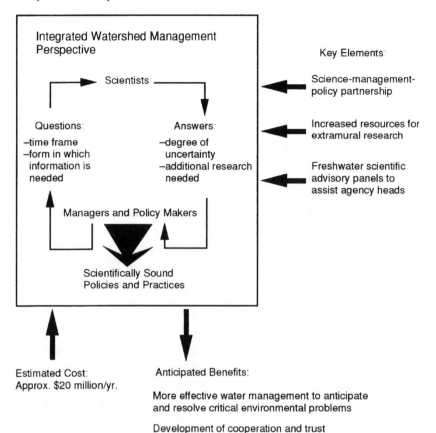

Figure 5.3   New Management Paradigms

tion to these answers and to support continuous research toward better answers. A third component of this effort is incorporation of government policy-making mechanisms into the process. Decision makers and land managers must base their actions to protect aquatic resources on scientifically sound policy. Ecological research and management programs based on partnerships of science, policy, and management will contribute to the resolution of critical environmental problems. Furthermore, this partnership must be developed at the earliest possible stage of the process to ensure that the proper questions are addressed by an appropriate balance of scholarly disciplines. Finally, to ensure that policy and management decisions will be based on scientific insights, the three elements must function interactively from the outset of the program design process.

It is recommended that the proposed FWI research program be conducted as an integral part of government agencies' water regulation, monitoring, and protection activities in order to provide the fundamental science basis for new management paradigms. A significant fraction of the research program should be for education and training as well as for investigator-initiated research at academic institutions. Investigator-driven studies can enlighten decision makers when they encounter the surprises or crises of the future. Core programs such as this also ensure the long-term vitality of a science by providing for exploration along lines that may overturn existing dogmas and propel scientific break-throughs.

The approach of funding research as a proportion of mission-directed programs is not unprecedented. For example, 10 percent of the budget of the USGS's National Water Quality Assessment Program is currently al-located to the agency's intramural research program. This book advocates that this approach be expanded to fund extramural research as well, oc-curring within an interagency, coordinated research infrastructure.

The proportion of regulatory, protection, and monitoring programs in-vested in research should be determined by each agency during the on-going coordination process. This would have a powerful influence on the scientific community and ensure that trained professionals resolve issues.

The proposed freshwater scientific advisory panels would provide a communication link between agency heads, high-level administrators, and the research community. These panels would be charged with providing scientific advice in an interdisciplinary context to an agency administra-tion that may have a limited scientific background. This recommendation is essential for linking research to management and policy decisions at the national level. Linkages between scientists and managers would be also fostered at the working level as the integrated watershed management per-spective is promulgated and developed through agencies and the private sector.

Estimated Cost

The increased resources for extramural research and the enablement funding for the recommended partnerships and panels are estimated to cost approximately $20 million per year.

Anticipated Benefits

The integrated watershed management approach can be expected to pro-vide improved freshwater management that anticipates and resolves crit-ical environmental problems. An additional benefit will be development of cooperation and trust among institutions that have not commonly worked together in the past.

Institutional Support

Institutional support for the Freshwater Imperative should be provided by the following means:

- Enhancement of existing programs of government agencies with water resource responsibilities to support innovative research as well as technology development and transfer. Key elements of this effort should be provision of adequate equipment and technical capabilities for the field and laboratory and standardization of protocols.

- Establishment of regional institutions to provide for interdisciplinary analysis of issues on a regional basis by integrating human sciences and natural sciences and involving managers from government, academia, and the private sector.

- Initiation of a new National Science Foundation program to promote effective multidisciplinary research on a scale commensurate with the significance of the scientific issues in limnology.

Since 1980, resources supporting freshwater research in many federal agencies have dwindled or disappeared, and NSF funds have been unable to meet increased demand. Growing constraints faced by state- and university-based programs have led to a reduction in institutional capabilities and many incidences of budgetary trauma. Current trends suggest that aquatic science is facing a crisis. Will the nation have the capability to create the next generation of scientists and managers equipped to deal with the growing number and complexity of freshwater issues?

The collective institutional support recommendations herein would provide a strong support base to complement both the movement to new management paradigms already described and the intellectual and physical infrastructure recommendations made later in this chapter.

Enhancement of Existing Programs

It is recommended that existing programs be enhanced to provide adequate support for innovation through individual investigator-initiated research programs (figure 5.4). It is further recommended that existing programs be enhanced to provide sufficient support for technology development and transfer. Key elements of these recommendations are standardization of limnological protocols and provision of adequate equipment for freshwater research.

Limnological programs have contributed greatly to identification and solution of environmental problems—for example, the recovery of polluted eutrophic lakes (Edmondson 1970, 1991; Carpenter and Kitchell

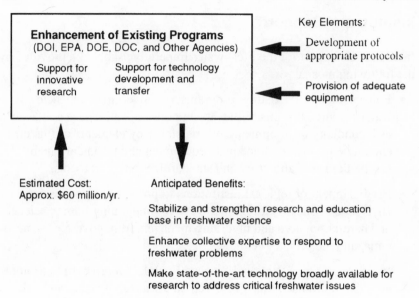

Figure 5.4   Enhancement of Existing Programs

1993), the discovery of acid rain as a U.S. problem (Likens, Bormann, and Johnson 1972), the effect of phosphate on lake eutrophication (Schindler 1974), the use of riparian corridors to maintain stream characteristics (Naiman and Décamps 1990) and the use wetlands to maintain water quality and biodiversity (National Research Council 1992). Research on water quality maintenance, sewage treatment, and control of waterborne disease has made enormous improvements to public health. And the nation's aquatic resource base has been enriched through research efforts in fisheries management and aquaculture.

Freshwater sciences face many challenges. Fragmentation of intellectual capital may result from the many distinct types of aquatic ecosystems encompassed by limnology. A focus on individual sites and types of water bodies has enriched our understanding of the diversity of natural freshwater ecosystems but may limit generalization to larger scales (Caraco, Cole, and Likens 1991). Freshwater science has only minimally contributed to an understanding of large-scale problems such as global climate change. Finally, limnological knowledge has been incompletely transferred to nonaquatic ecologists and land managers, who are, as a result, less able to apply their conceptual and methodological expertise to the solution of common research and management problems. Intellectual cross-fertilization between aquatic and terrestrial sciences thus has been somewhat asymmetrical.

Despite the shortcomings of the past, freshwater science is a vibrant, creative field that can make major contributions to the solution of current and future environmental crises. Enhancement of existing freshwater programs is fundamental for providing both stability for the field and the collective expertise needed to address current and emerging issues.

The technology required for comprehensive freshwater programs has become increasingly sophisticated and expensive. At present, progress in the field is limited by the availability of existing and advanced innovative technologies. Much of the instrumentation used in freshwater studies has been developed by the biomedical industry, has drawn from the analytical needs of regulatory agencies, or has been adapted from oceanography. Problems arise, however, in (1) generating capital to purchase new equipment and to develop advanced technologies suited for limnological applications, (2) obtaining funds to adapt existing technologies, and (3) supporting a critical balance of maintenance and technical staff.

The new scale of issues and demands for spatially explicit approaches requires development of new technologies that sample at larger scales. These and other new and advanced technologies must be complemented by standardization of methods, intercalibration, and improved capabilities for data verification and assessment. Limited funds in the freshwater sciences have often required individual investigators to adapt or build their own equipment. This has led to widespread use of multiple methods to make various measurements and collect samples. Workshops and intercalibration studies are necessary to standardize methods and to train freshwater scientists in the best techniques for sampling and measuring aquatic ecosystems. Standardization is also critical to the success of comparative limnology now and in the future (Cole, Lovett, and Findlay, 1991).

Freshwater scientists are seriously underequipped to perform the tasks at hand because of (1) aging and obsolescent equipment and facilities, (2) inadequate transfer of existing technology to limnology due to difficulties in modifying and adapting equipment to specific field situations, and (3) inadequate capital funding of research. In many cases, limited distribution of equipment has maintained a high per-unit cost. Increased capital investment will produce a substantial economy of scale.

Estimated Cost   The program enhancements envisaged here will cost approximately $60 million per year.

Anticipated Benefits   Enhancement of existing programs will stabilize and strengthen the research and education base in freshwater science while improving the nation's collective expertise to respond to freshwater problems. Another benefit of program enhancement will be to make state-of-the-art technology broadly available for research that can address critical freshwater issues.

Establishment of Regional Institutions

People have questions about freshwater resources that are regional in scale. Therefore, regional information is needed to set policy and to manage freshwater resources. Unfortunately, spatially explicit regional models that focus on movement of water and its dissolved, suspended, and biological loads are currently only coarsely developed. Yet these models are essential to understanding ecological processes at a scale at which humans interact with resources. Such an understanding will greatly enhance watershed management.

Development of regional models requires an understanding of water movement through all ecosystem components: groundwater and surface water, soils, lakes and streams, and linkages with the atmosphere and with recipient estuaries, water supplies, or aquifers. This scale of resolution is larger than typical NSF Long-Term Ecological Research (LTER) sites or the UNESCO Man and the Biosphere (MAB) reserves—although it can and should include several. The information generated will describe a sufficiently diverse and heterogeneous system to allow scaling up to continental or global scales. Process-based understanding of regional ecosystems will require ecological studies at scales ranging from the molecular to the landscape.

It is recommended that a network of six regionally focused cooperative institutions be established for interdisciplinary analysis of issues by experts in the social sciences, the natural sciences, and the management sciences and engineering (figure 5.5). These institutions should be developed within academic and nongovernmental institutions. Scientists, managers, and engineers should come from federal and state government, academia, and the private sector. Regions should be based on hydrologically or climatologically defined drainages, should incorporate human activities, and should be substantially larger than traditional LTER sites. Examples might be the Hudson River, Savannah River, and Columbia River basins, the Sacramento–San Joaquin (Central Valley) basin, the Great Lakes basin, and Chesapeake Bay. Or the regional centers could focus on ecoregions such as western temperate rain forests, the Great Plains, or eastern subtropical deciduous forests. Although regional studies of various kinds are currently under way, none is primarily focused on water issues or pursued from a viewpoint of predicting the consequences of environmental change.

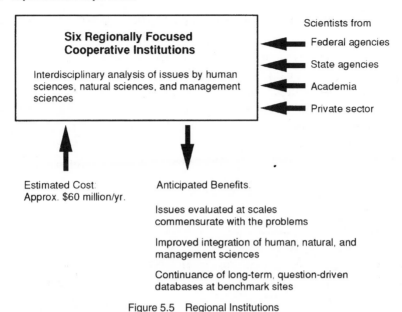

Figure 5.5   Regional Institutions

It is further recommended that experimental and modeling components be incorporated at established long-term sites that are now dedicated primarily to monitoring activities. This would require an infusion of research funds, logically from the agencies now administering these sites or networks of sites supported by the DOE, the NSF, the DOI, and others. In addition, the establishment of a National Center for Environmental Analysis and Synthesis is supported (Ecological Society of America and Association of Ecosystem Research Centers 1993), and it is recommended that a freshwater component be specifically included in this center.

Estimated Cost   Each regional institution is estimated to cost approximately $10 million per year, for a total of $60M million per year. It is suggested that initial funding should be for four years, with biennial reviews thereafter.

Anticipated Benefits   The strength of the regional institutions will be the in capability to evaluate issues at a scale commensurate with the problems. These institutions will also improve integration of the human, natural, and management sciences and ensure the continuance of long-term question-driven databases at benchmark monitoring sites.

An Integrated National Science Foundation Program

Lake, stream, and wetland scientists engaged in fundamental research find that the NSF's institutional structure does not conform to the scope and dimensions of their science (Firth and Wyngaard 1993). Aquatic systems present themselves for study as features of the earth, complete with geophysical and chemical aspects in addition to organisms. Compelling and potentially revealing lines of inquiry about these systems could be conducted purely on geological, physical, chemical, or biological levels. Nevertheless, there are also inquiries that could focus rewardingly on interfaces between any two disciplines or on further amalgamations.

By reason of the nation's need to ensure the existence of a vibrant pool of creative scientists for future exigencies, it is strongly recommended that the NSF nurture an integrated program in freshwater science (figure 5.6). The NSF might consider an experimental interdivisional program with budgetary authority and the mandate to evaluate and review multidisciplinary proposals.

Furthermore, this interdivisional program should be assisted by an Advisory Committee on Inland Waters composed of scientists and managers who serve on a rotating basis and assist the program in developing strategic initiatives and long-range plans. This program should be carefully formulated to ensure a broad disciplinary perspective and should have both research and facilities sections. Cooperation between the geosciences and biological sciences directorates is necessary for success with this program. Involvement of the engineering, mathematical and physical sciences, and social, behavioral, and economic directorates would enhance the program. Full implementation of this recommendation requires additional resources for the NSF. Funding should not be reallocated from current NSF programs.

Freshwater scientists can and should be closely involved in defining the directions in which their field develops. Identifying and fine-tuning the balance between directed research and investigator-initiated research requires a continuing effort involving the breadth of the profession. It is important for limnology to define carefully its scientific objectives and to maintain this focus as partnerships are developed with management agencies, public and private groups, and other government sectors with their own individual objectives. As aquatic science properly increases its contribution to the solution of societal issues, it must remain vigilant in maintaining the vibrant core of fundamental science on which the entire enterprise rests.

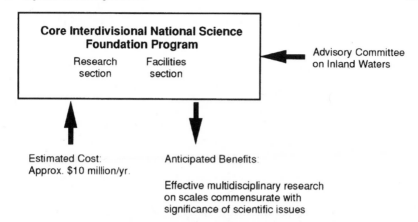

Figure 5.6   An Integrated National Science Foundation Program

Estimated Cost   The integrated National Science Foundation program is estimated to cost approximately $10 million per year. It is reiterated that funding should *not* be reallocated from current NSF programs.

Anticipated Benefits   The integrated NSF program will provide much-needed support for fundamental research in freshwater sciences and will make possible effective multidisciplinary research on scales commensurate with the significance of the scientific and social issues.

Physical and Intellectual Research Infrastructure

The physical and intellectual infrastructure for the Freshwater Imperative should be enhanced through the following:

- Establishment of a Freshwater Biodiversity Center to provide systematic and comprehensive data on freshwater biodiversity, develop sensitive biotic indices of environmental change, and enhance predictability and accuracy in monitoring programs.

- Establishment of an array of long-term and altered research sites with specific freshwater emphases.

- Strengthening of education and communication to provide for innovative and broad-based training for students and professionals in the freshwater sciences beyond traditional efforts already under way in academia, national laboratories, and private institutions. This would include, for example, support for continuing education and "retooling" for mid-career scientists and managers, workshops on newly evolving technologies and concepts, and cooperative public and private sector training grants.

Establishment of a Freshwater Biodiversity Center

Understanding the relationships between biodiversity and ecosystem processes will be a major research focus requiring thorough analysis of species relationships. The Freshwater Biodiversity Center will provide information concerning species, their distributions, and their habitats that will be essential in detecting influences of environmental change on the sustainability of freshwater ecosystems (figure 5.7). National monitoring and assessment programs cooperating with the center can also aid in documenting human effects on ecosystem dynamics. From the basic science perspective, enhanced taxonomic understanding will advance our knowledge of food web structure, phenotypic variability, and adaptation to environmental change. Improved phylogenetic analyses will permit historical interpretation and prediction of yet-unknown ecological phenomena.

The mission of the Freshwater Biodiversity Center will be to coordinate and facilitate research on freshwater biological and habitat diversity. It should be supported by such agencies as the National Biological Service (DOI), the EPA, and the NSF and will be composed of five facilities, each with a unique but complementary task:

- The Biological Data Facility will compile and make available data on North American freshwater biotas, including systematics collections.

- The Environmental Assessment Facility will provide a national habitat inventory at selected sites as appropriate.

- The Molecular and Biochemical Systematics Facility will assist in the transfer of new technologies for taxonomic and systematics research. Molecular characterization of species and association of insect larvae (mostly aquatic) with their adult forms (mostly terrestrial) will be a primary objective, followed by phylogenetic investigations and subsequent interpretive and predictive analyses.

- The Computer Imaging Facility will provide a central resource to facilitate compilation of electronic monographs and images.

- The Cryogenic Conservation Facility will develop methods and serve as a site for long-term preservation of endangered freshwater organisms.

Estimated Cost   The Freshwater Biodiversity Center is projected to cost approximately $15 million per year.

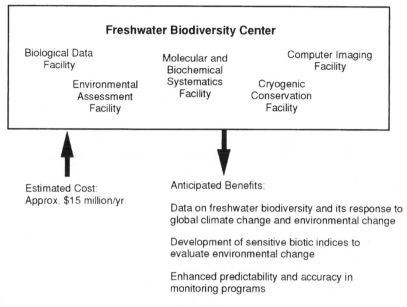

Figure 5.7   Freshwater Biodiversity Center

Anticipated Benefits   The Freshwater Biodiversity Center will be expected to provide data on freshwater biodiversity and its response to global climate change and other major environmental changes. The center will also develop sensitive biotic indices to evaluate environmental change and enhance predictability and accuracy in monitoring programs.

Establishment of Coordinated Research Sites

A broad array of coordinated sites will be essential for investigating the priority research areas identified in this book. These research sites should include those that are relatively pristine and functioning in a natural state as well as those in which human activities control or significantly affect ecosystem function. An understanding of basic mechanisms that control fluxes and transport of materials and toxins in freshwater is essential to managing water quality, quantity, and productivity. In collaboration with the Freshwater Biodiversity Center, a coordinated network of research sites can enhance understanding of the relationship of biodiversity to ecosystem processes.

It is recommended that this network of freshwater research sites be established primarily by incorporating and building on sites currently studied by government agencies and academic institutions. An organized interagency process for building this network and for augmenting sites to attain a base level of instrumentation and monitoring is essential for the conduct of future comparative studies. Augmentation of studies for research sites could be funded competitively within a given agency and could include support for collaborating academic scientists.

Benefits derived from comparative studies within this network of sites could be further strengthened by coordination with similar networks in Canada, Europe, and other regions. Expansion of the scale of this comparative research will help determine the effects of human activities on environmental variables such as biodiversity. Contrasts among habitats and among regions where different human-derived legacies dominate landscapes will also provide an approach to measuring relative values of freshwater resources.

The goal of the coordinated research sites will be to integrate understanding of existing legacies, ongoing processes, and experimental perturbation in order to gain a predictive understanding of change in fresh waters. Whenever possible, sites should contain a variety of aquatic habitats, such as springs, streams, wetlands, lakes, and reservoirs. Experimental restoration of affected habitats together with evaluation research (see figure 3.1) will be undertaken to test directly the progress being made toward understanding.

In addition to maintaining the existing array of freshwater research sites in the United States, two unique types of long-term research sites are required to capture the spatial and temporal scales of freshwater issues (figure 5.8). The first are long-term research sites with a freshwater emphasis placed, for example, around such bodies of water as large lakes, freshwater wetlands, large rivers, and reservoirs. There should be at least five additional networked sites, such as NSF Long-Term Ecological Research (LTER) sites or DOE National Environmental Research Parks (NERPs), which focus on aquatic systems. (Although approximately half of the current LTER sites incorporate an aquatic component, only two or three are primarily aquatic.) The program should also add two long-term sites linked to major drainage basins, lakes, or reservoirs, such as the Great Lakes, Colorado River, upper Columbia River, or Mississippi River.

The other type of site would be on severely degraded or disturbed systems, such as physically altered systems, systems with toxic contamination, and urban lakes and streams. Research sites are needed in these cases to understand cumulative effects as we separate human-caused from natural variabilities and to provide fundamental insights into system dynamics.

Estimated Cost   Implementation of the recommendations for research sites is projected to cost approximately $20 million per year.

Research Sites

Long-term Research Sites with
Freshwater Emphases:

  –Large lakes
  –Freshwater wetlands
  –Large rivers
  –Reservoirs

Research Sites on Severely
Degraded or Disturbed Systems:

  –Physically altered systems
  –Systems with toxic contamination
  –Urban lakes and streams

Estimated Cost:
Approx. $20 million/yr.

Anticipated Benefits:

Ability to examine linkages between human activities
and biological legacies

Ability to address questions of human sustainability
and linkages between science and management

Understanding of how severely altered environments
respond to and recover from chemical, physical, and
biotic perturbations

Figure 5.8   Research Sites

Anticipated Benefits   The proposed network of research sites will improve our ability to examine linkages between human activities and biotic legacies, as well as our ability to address questions of human sustainability and the linkages between science and management. In addition, we will obtain an improved understanding of how severely altered environments respond to and recover from chemical, physical, and biotic perturbations.

Strengthened Education and Communication

Human resources provide the cornerstone for intellectual vigor. In the field of limnology, the educational, training, and communication systems require strengthening (figure 5.9). In particular, long-term continuity of education and training efforts should be improved for professional scientists and managers. Freshwater science has benefited from surges of interest that accompanied efforts to deal with eutrophication in the 1970s and acid precipitation in the 1980s. But the field consistently fails to attract and support the best students and to maintain and update training for practicing aquatic scientists, technicians, and managers. The following specific recommendations are suggested:

- Support and maintain centers and field stations with diverse expertise in freshwater science, especially those with intensive curricula in limnology and allied areas, to upgrade education of students and scientists with a primary interest in management.

- Establish cooperative training grants for graduate and postdoctoral education in freshwater science. These grants could be supported by agencies that expect to make increasing use of limnologists and ecosystem scientists in the future.

- Develop continuing education and retraining programs for agency personnel and others to meet the rapidly changing demands of the field. Special provisions must be made to accommodate the retraining needs of workers displaced by environmental change.

- Increase funding for interdisciplinary conferences and workshops involving scientists from disparate fields of freshwater and allied sciences. These might be modeled after the Gordon conferences and should focus on holistic approaches to resolving contemporary and emerging issues.

- Increase efforts to communicate scientific information to laypersons, reporters, and science writers. Also, communicate the potential problem-solving role of freshwater science to management and funding agencies, legislators, and the general public, as the NOAA Sea Grant Program already does for the Great Lakes and other regions. Public relations efforts in limnology have been underdeveloped, uncoordinated, and unfocused. Perhaps a Freshwater Science Council, with representatives from professional societies, conservation groups, and industrial consortia, could be developed to take a unified active role in this effort. An educated and informed electorate is critical to both the economic development and the environmental sustainability of the nation in an increasingly complex world.

- Enhance managers' access to scientific information. Communication is a central ingredient of the FWI. Too frequently, managers must make decisions in a time frame that prevents them from accumulating all the information necessary or desirable to make effective decisions. A partnership of managers, policy makers, and scientists is essential to best utilize existing information in an atmosphere that includes clear communication of risks and ecological values yet embodies trust and respect. Managers require reliable sources of information and mechanisms for obtaining it; implementation of the FWI will provide for these needs.

- Support training workshops and programs for specific, newly evolving technologies and concepts, such as GIS-CAD models, land-

---

Strengthened Education and Communication

Training workshops for new and evolving technologies and concepts	Funding for interdisciplinary workshops focused on crosscutting issues
Limnological curricula to educate people with primarily management interests	Improved public relations on the role of limnological expertise in solving environmental problems
Continuing education and retraining efforts for agency personnel	Cooperative training grants for graduate and postdoctoral education

Estimated Cost:
Approx. $15 million/yr.

Anticipated Benefits:

Training for young professionals; education and retraining of existing work force

Improved communication among researchers, managers, policy makers, and the public

Communication of science to laypersons

Stability of "pipeline" supplying limnologists for management agencies and other decision-making organizations

Figure 5.9 Strengthened Education and Communication

scape ecology, remote sensing, and molecular systematics. Training programs increase an individual's ability to compete in the job market; collectively, this competitiveness will determine the nation's success in international markets.

Estimated Cost This element of the proposed education and communication recommendation is projected to cost approximately $15 million per year.

Anticipated Benefits The strengthened education and communication portions of the program will provide specialized training for young professionals and education or retraining of the existing work force; improved communication among researchers, managers, policy makers, and the public; training of science writers and reporters; communication of science to laypersons; and stability of the "pipeline" supplying freshwater scientists to management agencies and other decision-making organizations.

Closing Remarks

Changes in the distribution, abundance, and quality of water and freshwater resources in this century represent a strategic threat to the quality of human life, the environmental sustainability of the biosphere, and the viability of human cultures. As a result, scientists and managers are increasingly called on to provide a predictive understanding of freshwater ecosystems but are unable to respond at a scale commensurate with the issues. Achieving a predictive understanding will require effective integration of science and management as well as development of unambiguous criteria for making management and policy decisions.

It is widely recognized that a number of fundamental deficiencies exist in our national infrastructure supporting freshwater sciences and management: inability to predict future vitality of altered environments, to combine environmental and socioeconomic sciences into an integrated ecosystem perspective, and to provide a national research and education infrastructure that allows an effective response to emerging issues. The Freshwater Imperative research agenda, framed by science issues with immediate policy relevance, describes a fundamental program to help ensure that today's uncertainties do not become tomorrow's problems. Freshwater ecosystems play a central role in our nation's social, economic, environmental, and political mosaic. Yet the scope of water-related issues often exceeds the capacity of individual disciplines, institutions, or governments to resolve them.

A primary goal of the Freshwater Imperative is to assist in the development of a national strategy for freshwater science and management. The FWI research agenda and its implementation are recommendations made by members of the nation's freshwater scientific community to ensure that water resource managers and policy makers have adequate and timely information to protect, utilize, and enhance water resources. The FWI identifies high-priority research areas and proposes a conceptual framework for building a durable infrastructure that will prepare the United States to deal with the issues of the twenty-first century. It is recognized that improvements will be made as the FWI is implemented; however, it is also recognized that a comprehensive, integrated freshwater program is urgently needed if the nation is eventually to resolve water-related issues in a realistic manner. The program outlined in this book is an important step in that direction.

FWI Research Agenda Participants

The intent of the Freshwater Imperative process was to produce a limnological research agenda accurately reflecting the needs and challenges that the entire field of freshwater science and management will face in the decades to come. To obtain the requisite broad-based perspective, the process included the judgments of a multidisciplinary team of the nation's leading freshwater scientists. To be a credible and effective tool in freshwater policy and management, the FWI research agenda embraced the controversy and scope of perspectives inevitable in such a broad research area. Furthermore, while the recommendations set out in the FWI are meant to stand on their own, this book would be incomplete if it overlooked the context from which they emerged. Finally, and most important, this appendix specifically acknowledges the scientists and managers who took the time and accepted the responsibility to contribute to the creation of the Freshwater Imperative research agenda.

Steering Committee

ROBERT J. NAIMAN, Co-chair
Center for Streamside Studies, AR-10
University of Washington
Seattle, Wash. 98195

JOHN J. MAGNUSON, Co-chair
Center for Limnology
University of Wisconsin
Madison, Wis. 53711

G. RONNIE BEST
Center for Wetlands and Water Resources
University of Florida
Gainesville, Fla. 32611

ELIZABETH R. BLOOD
Joseph W. Jones Ecological
    Research Center
Newton, Ga. 29208

PENELOPE FIRTH
Ex officio
National Science Foundation
Arlington, Va. 22230

NELSON G. HAIRSTON JR.
Section of Ecology and Systematics
Cornell University
Ithaca, N.Y. 14853

GENE E. LIKENS
Institute of Ecosystem Studies
Millbrook, N.Y. 12545

SALLY MACINTYRE
Marine Sciences Institute
University of California
Santa Barbara, Calif. 93106

DIANE M. MCKNIGHT
U.S. Geological Survey
Boulder, Colo. 80303

JACK A. STANFORD
Flathead Lake Biological Station
University of Montana
Polson, Mont. 59860

JEFFREY E. RICHEY
School of Oceanography
University of Washington
Seattle, Wash. 98195

ROBERT G. WETZEL
Department of Biological Sciences
University of Alabama
Tuscaloosa, Ala. 35487

1993 Workshop Participants

Roger Blair
Environmental Research Laboratory
Environmental Protection Agency
Corvallis, Oreg. 97330

Stephen B. Brandt
Chesapeake Biological Laboratory
University of Maryland
Solomons, Md. 20688

Stephanie A. Cirillo
Sustainable Biosphere Initiative
Washington, D.C. 20036

Alan P. Covich
Department of Fishery and
   Wildlife Biology
Colorado State University
Fort Collins, Colo. 80523

Clifford N. Dahm
Department of Biology
University of New Mexico
Albuquerque, N.M. 87131

Henri Décamps
Centre d'Ecologie des Systems
   Fluviaux
Centre National de la
   Recherche Scientifique
31055 Toulouse, France

W. Thomas Edmondson
Department of Zoology, NJ-15
University of Washington
Seattle, Wash. 98195

Everett J. Fee
Freshwater Institute
Department of Fisheries and Oceans
Winnipeg, Manitoba, Canada R3T 2N6

Stuart G. Fisher
Department of Zoology
Arizona State University
Tempe, Ariz. 85287

James R. Gosz
Division of Environmental Biology
National Science Foundation
Washington, D.C. 20550

Richard A. Haeuber
Sustainable Biosphere Initiative
Washington, D.C. 20036

Paul D. N. Hebert
Department of Zoology
University of Guelph
Guelph, Ontario, Canada N1G 2W1

John E. Hobbie
The Ecosystems Center
Marine Biological Laboratory
Woods Hole, Mass. 02543

Robert W. Howarth
Section of Ecology and Systematics
Cornell University
Ithaca, N.Y.14853

Carol A. Johnston
Natural Resources Research Institute
University of Minnesota
Duluth, Minn. 55811

James R. Karr
Institute for Environmental Studies, FM-12
University of Washington
Seattle, Wash. 98195

Robert H. Kennedy
Environmental Laboratory
U.S. Army Corps of Engineers
Vicksburg, Miss. 39180

Dan B. Kimball
Water Resources Division, N.P.S.
U.S. Department of the Interior
Denver, Colo. 80225

James F. Kitchell
Center for Limnology
University of Wisconsin
Madison, Wis. 52706

Robert T. Lackey
Center for Analysis of
   Environmental Change
Oregon State University
Corvallis, Oreg. 97333

Winfried Lampert
Max Planck Institute for Limnology
2320 Plön, Germany

John T. Lehman
Department of Biology
University of Michigan
Ann Arbor, Mich. 48109

William M. Lewis Jr.
Center for Limnology
University of Colorado
Boulder, Colo. 30309

G. Richard Marzolf
U.S. Geological Survey
Denver, Colo. 80225

Judy L. Meyer
Department of Ecology
University of Georgia
Athens, Ga. 30602

John C. Morse
Department of Entomology
Clemson University
Clemson, S.C. 29634

Peter B. Moyle
Wildlife and Fisheries Biology
University of California
Davis, Calif. 95616

Michael L. Pace
Institute of Ecosystem Studies
Millbrook, N.Y. 12545

Bruce J. Peterson
The Ecosystems Center
Marine Biological Laboratory
Woods Hole, Mass. 02543

Geoffrey E. Petts
School of Geography
University of Birmingham
Edgbaston, Birmingham, England B15 2TT

Mary E. Power
Department of Integrative Biology
University of California
Berkeley, Calif. 94720

Catherine M. Pringle
Department of Ecology
University of Georgia
Athens, Ga. 30602

Rebecca R. Sharitz
Savannah River Ecology Laboratory
Aiken, S.C. 29802

Robin L. Welcomme
Inland Water Resources and
    Aquaculture Service
U. N. Food and Agriculture Organization
00100 Rome, Italy

Books and Proceedings Reviewed by the FWI Steering Committee

As part of the process of developing the Freshwater Imperative research agenda, the FWI Steering Committee reviewed recent books and proceedings of national and international workshops related to the status, trends, and future of freshwaters. Twenty-one documents were examined, individual summaries were prepared, and key recommendations were identified. These books and proceedings were reviewed to ensure that the FWI research agenda covered the broadest possible spectrum of freshwater issues, reflected extensive input from the limnological community, and explicitly linked research, management, and policy. The books and proceedings are acknowledged here because of their important contributions in informing the FWI process and to give readers the opportunity to understand the context from which the FWI research agenda grew.

Carpenter, S. R., ed. 1988. *Complex ecological interactions in lake communities.* New York: Springer-Verlag.

Dale, V. H., R. H. Gardner, and M. Turner. 1989. Predicting across scales: Theory development and testing. *Landscape Ecology* 3:147–255.

Drake, J. A., H. A. Mooney, F. di Castri, R. H. Groves, F. J. Kruger, M. Rejmánek, and M. Williamson, eds. 1989. *Biological invasions: A global perspective. SCOPE 37.* New York: Wiley .

Edmonson, W. T. 1991. *The uses of ecology: Lake Washington and beyond.* Seattle: University of Washington Press.

Firth, P., and S. G. Fisher, eds. 1991. *Global climate change and freshwater ecosystems.* New York: Springer-Verlag.

Hairston, N. G. Jr., P. Hebert, D. Lonsdale, N. Marcus, L. Weider, G. Wyngaard, M. Boileau, S. Dodson, and W. C. Kerfoot. n.d Genetics, evolution, and systematics. Chap. 2 in *Zooplankton biology,* edited by A. J. Tessier and C. Goulden. Princeton University Press.

Houghton, J. T., G. J. Jenkins, and J. J. Ephraums, eds. 1990. *Climate change: The scientific assessment.* Cambridge: Cambridge University Press.

Lehman, J. T., ed. 1986. *Basic issues in Great Lakes research,* Special Report no. 12. Ann Arbor: University of Michigan, Great Lakes Research Division.

Lubchenco, J., A. M. Olson, L. B. Brubaker, S. R. Carpenter, M. M. Holland, S. P. Hubbell, S. A. Levin, J. A. MacMahon, P. A. Matson, J. M. Melillo, H. A. Mooney, C. H. Peterson, H. R. Pulliam, L. A. Real, P. J. Regal, and P. G. Risser. 1991. The sustainable biosphere initiative: An ecological research agenda. *Ecology* 72:371–412.

Naiman, R. J., ed. 1992. *Watershed management: Balancing sustainability and environmental change.* New York: Springer-Verlag.

Naiman, R. J., and H. Décamps, eds. 1990. *The ecology and management of aquatic-terrestrial ecotones.* Man and the Biosphere Series no. 4. Paris: UNESCO; Carnforth, England: Parthenon.

National Aeronautics and Space Administration. 1988. *From pattern to process: The strategy of the earth observing system.* EOS Science Steering Committee Report, vol. 2. Washington, D.C.: National Aeronautics and Space Administration.

National Research Council. 1991. *Opportunities in the hydrologic sciences.* Washington, D.C.: National Academy Press.

———. 1992. *Restoration of aquatic ecosystems: Science, technology, and the public.* Washington, D.C.: National Academy Press.

Regier, H. A., J. J. Magnuson, and C. C. Coutant. 1990. Symposium on effects of climate change on fish. *Transactions of the American Fisheries Society* 119:173–389.

Risser, P. G., ed. 1991. *Long-term ecological research: An international perspective. SCOPE 47.* New York: Wiley.

Solbrig, O. T., and G. Nicholas, eds. 1991. *From genes to ecosystems: A research agenda for biodiversity.* Cambridge, Mass.: International Union of Biological Sciences.

Stanford, J. A., and A. P. Covich, eds. 1988. Community structure and function in temperate and tropical streams. *Journal of the North American Benthological Society* 7:261–529.

Systematics Agenda 2000. 1994. *Systematics Agenda 2000: Charting the biosphere.* New York: Systematics Agenda.

Turner II, B. L., W. C. Clark, R. W. Kates, J. F. Richards, J. T. Mathews, and W. B. Meyer, eds. 1993. *The earth as transformed by human action: Global and regional changes in the biosphere over the past 300 years.* Cambridge: Cambridge University Press.

U.S. Department of Agriculture. 1992. *Water resource challenges and opportunities for the 21st century.* Washington, D.C.: U.S. Department of Agriculture.

Water Environment Federation. 1992. *Water Quality 2000 final report : A national agenda for the 21st century.* Publication no. TT02. Alexandria, Va.: Water Environment Federation.

Literature Cited

Anderson, D. M., S. B. Galloway, and J. D. Joseph. 1992. *Marine biotoxins and harmful algae: A national plan.* Technical Report no. WHOI-93-02. Woods Hole, Mass.: Woods Hole Oceanographic Institution.

Anderson, M. P., and C. J. Bowser. 1986. The role of groundwater in delaying lake acidification. *Water Resources Research* 22:1101–1108.

Bellrose, F. C. 1980. *Ducks, geese, and swans of North America.* Harrisburg, Pa.: Stackpole.

Benke, A. C. 1990. A perspective on America's vanishing streams. *Journal of the North American Benthological Society* 9:77–88.

Bennett, J. W., and K. A. Dahlberg. 1990. Institutions, social organization, and cultural values. In *The earth as transformed by human action: Global and regional changes in the biosphere over the past 300 years,* edited by B. L. Turner II, W. C. Clark, R. W. Kates, J. F. Richards, J. T. Mathews, and W. B. Meyer, 69–86. Cambridge: Cambridge University Press.

Berry, B. J. 1990. Urbanization. In *The earth as transformed by human action: Global and regional changes in the biosphere over the past 300 years,* edited by B. L. Turner II, W. C. Clark, R. W. Kates, J. F. Richards, J. T. Mathews, and W. B. Meyer, 103–119. Cambridge: Cambridge University Press.

Bisson, P. A., T. P. Quinn, G. H. Reeves, and S. V. Gregory. 1992. Best management practices, cumulative effects, and long-term trends in fish abundance in Pacific Northwest river systems. In *Watershed management: Balancing sustainability and environmental change,* edited by R. J. Naiman, 189–232. New York: Springer-Verlag.

Bloom, N. G., C. J. Waters, and J. P. Hurley. 1991. Impact of acidification on the methylmercury cycling of remote seepage lakes. *Water, Air, and Soil Pollution* 50:477–492.

Bodaly, R. A., R. E. Hecky, and R. J. P. Fudge. 1984. Increases in fish mercury levels in lakes flooded by the Churchill River diversion, Northern Manitoba. *Canadian Journal of Fisheries and Aquatic Sciences* 41:682–691.

Bogan, A. E. 1995. Freshwater bivalve extinctions. *American Zoologist.* In press.

Bothwell, M. L., D. Sherbot, A. C. Roberge, and R. J. Daley. 1993. Influence of natural ultraviolet radiation on lotic periphytic diatom community growth, biomass accrual, and species composition: Short-term versus long-term effects. *Journal of Phycology* 29:24–35.

Botkin, D. B. 1990. *Discordant harmonies.* New York: Oxford University Press.

Britton, L. J., K. E. Goddard, and J. C. Briggs. 1983. *Quality of rivers of the United States,*

1976 water year—based on the National Stream Quality Accounting Network (NASQAN). Open-File Report no. 80-594. Denver: U.S. Geological Survey.

Bubeck, R. C., W. H. Diment, B. L. Deck, A. L. Baldwin, and S. D. Lipton. 1971. Runoff of deicing salt: Effect on Irondequoit Bay, Rochester, New York. *Science* 172:1128–1131.

Calow, P., and G. E. Petts, eds. 1992. *Rivers handbook: Hydrological and ecological processes.* Cambridge, Mass.: Blackwell.

Caraco, N., J. J. Cole, and G. E. Likens. 1991. Cross-system study of phosphorus release from lake sediments. In *Comparative analyses of ecosystems: Patterns, mechanisms, and theories,* edited by J. J. Cole, G. Lovett, and S. Findlay, 241–258. New York: Springer-Verlag.

Carlton, J. T. 1989. Man's role in changing the face of the ocean: Biological invasions and implications for conservation of near-shore environments. *Conservation Biology* 3:265–273.

Carpenter, S. R., ed. 1988. *Complex ecological interactions in lake communities.* New York: Springer-Verlag.

Carpenter, S. R. 1992. Destabilization of planktonic ecosystems and blooms of blue-green algae. In *Food web management: A case study of Lake Mendota,* edited by J. F. Kitchell, 461–481. New York: Springer-Verlag.

Carpenter, S. R., S. G. Fisher, N. B. Grimm, and J. F. Kitchell. 1992. Global change and freshwater ecosystems. *Annual Review of Ecology and Systematics* 23:119–139.

Carpenter, S. R., and J. F. Kitchell, eds. 1993. *The trophic cascade in lakes.* Cambridge: Cambridge University Press.

Carpenter, S. R., J. F. Kitchell, and J. R. Hodgson. 1985. Cascading trophic interactions and lake productivity. *BioScience* 35:634–639.

Carson, R. 1962. *Silent spring.* Boston: Houghton Mifflin.

Charles, D. F. 1991. *Acidic deposition and aquatic ecosystems: Regional case studies.* New York: Springer-Verlag.

Chisholm, M. 1990. The increasing separation of production and consumption. In *The earth as transformed by human action: Global and regional changes in the biosphere over the past 300 years,* edited by B. L. Turner II, W. C. Clark, R. W. Kates, J. F. Richards, J. T. Mathews, and W. B. Meyer, 87–101. Cambridge: Cambridge University Press.

Christmas, J., and C. de Rooy. 1991. The decade and beyond at a glance. *Water International* 16:127–134.

Clark, C. W. 1991. Economic biases against sustainable development. In *Ecological economics: The science and management of sustainability,* edited by R. Costanza, 319–330. New York: Columbia University Press.

Colborn, T. E., and C. Clement. 1992. Chemically induced alterations in sexual and functional development: The wildlife-human connection. In vol. 21 of *Advances in modern environmental toxicology.* Princeton, N.J.: Princeton Scientific.

Colborn, T. E., A. Davidson, S. N. Green, R. A. Hodge, C. I. Jackson, and R. A. Liroff. 1990. *Great Lakes, great legacy?* Washington, D.C.: Conservation Foundation.

Cole, J. J., G. Lovett, and S. Findlay, eds. 1991. *Comparative analyses of ecosystems: Patterns, mechanisms, and theories.* New York: Springer-Verlag.

Cole, J. J., B. L. Peierls, N. F. Caraco, and M. L. Pace. 1993. Nitrogen loading of rivers as a human-driven process. In *Humans as components of ecosystems,* edited by M. J. McDonnell and S. T. A. Pickett, 141–157. New York: Springer-Verlag.

Covich, A. P., T. A. Crowl, E. L. Johnson, D. Varza, and D. L. Certain. 1991. Post–Hurricane Hugo increases in atyid shrimp abundances in a Puerto Rican montane stream. *Biotropica* 23:448–454.

Craig, J. F., and J. B. Kemper, eds. 1987. *Regulated streams: Advances in ecology.* New York: Plenum Press.

Cross, F. B., and R. E. Moss. 1987. Historic changes in fish communities and aquatic habitats in plains streams of Kansas. In *Community and evolutionary ecology of North American stream fishes,* edited by W. J. Matthews and D. C. Heins, 155–165. Norman: University of Oklahoma Press.

Culver, D. A. 1975. Physical, chemical, and biological factors in the initiation and destruction of biogenic meromixis in a soft-water lake. *Verhandlungen Internationale Vereinigung für Theoretische und Angewandte Limnologie* 19:776–783.

Culver, D. A., R. M. Vaga, C. S. Munch, and S. M. Harris. 1981. Paleoecology of Hall Lake, Washington: A history of meromixis and disturbance. *Ecology* 62:848–863.

Dahl, T. E. 1990. *Wetlands losses in the United States, 1780s to 1980s.* Washington, D.C.: U.S. Department of the Interior, Fish and Wildlife Service.

Dar, E., M. S. Kanarak, H. A. Anderson, and W. C. Sonzogni. 1992. Fish consumption and reproductive outcomes in Green Bay, Wisconsin. *Environmental Research* 59:189–201.

Décamps, H., and R. J. Naiman. 1989. L'Ecologie des fleuves. *La Recherche* 20:310–318.

Degens, E. T., S. Kempe, and J. E. Richey. 1991. *Biogeochemistry of major world rivers.* New York: Wiley.

Detenbeck, N. E., C. A. Johnston, and G. J. Niemi. 1993. Wetland effects on lake water quality in the Minneapolis/St. Paul metropolitan area. *Landscape Ecology* 8:39–61.

Dodds, W. K. 1991. Micro-environmental charactistics of filamentous algal communities in flowing freshwaters. *Freshwater Biology* 25:199–209.

Dynesius, M., and C. Nilsson. 1994. Fragmentation and flow regulation of river systems in the northern third of the world. *Science* 266: 753–762.

Ebel, W. J., C. D. Becker, J. W. Mullan, and H. L. Raymond. 1989. The Columbia River: Toward a holistic understanding. In *Proceedings of the International Large Rivers Symposium,* edited by D. P. Dodge, 205–219. Ottawa, Canada: Department of Fisheries and Oceans.

Ecological Society of America and Association of Ecosystem Research Centers. 1993. *National Center for Ecological Synthesis: Scientific objectives, structure, and implementation. Report to the National Science Foundation.* Washington, D.C.: Ecological Society of America; Woods Hole, Mass.: Association of Ecosystems Research Centers.

Edmondson, W. T. 1970. Phosphorus, nitrogen, and algae in Lake Washington after diversion of sewage. *Science* 169:690–691.

————. 1991. *The uses of ecology: Lake Washington and beyond.* Seattle: University of Washington Press.

————. 1994. What is limnology? In *Limnology now: A paradigm of planetary problems,* edited by R. Margalef, 547–553. New York: Elsevier.

Edmondson, W. T., and J. T. Lehman. 1981. The effect of changes in nutrient outcome on the condition of Lake Washington. *Limnology and Oceanography* 26:1–29.

Edwards, D. D. 1993. Troubled waters in Milwaukee. *American Society for Microbiology News* 59:342–345.

Ehrlich, P. R., and A. H. Ehrlich. 1990. *The population explosion.* New York: Simon and Schuster.

Ellner, S., and N. G. Hairston Jr. 1994. Role of overlapping generations in maintaining genetic variation in a fluctuating environment. *American Naturalist* 143:403–417.

Elwood, J. W., J. D. Newbold, R. V. O'Neill, and W. Van Winkle. 1983. Resource spiraling: An operational paradigm for analyzing lotic ecosystems. In *Dynamics of lotic ecosystems,* edited by T. D. Fontaine and S. M. Bartell, 3–27. Ann Arbor Mich.: Ann Arbor Scientific.

Engelman, R., and P. LeRoy. 1993. *Sustaining water.* Washington, D.C.: Population Action International.

Environmental Protection Agency. 1983. *Results of the Nationwide Urban Runoff Program: Executive summary.* Washington, D.C.: Government Printing Office.

————. 1991. *Environmental investments: The cost of a clean environment.* Washington, D.C.: Island Press.

Falkenmark, M. 1989. The massive water scarcity now threatening Africa–why isn't it being addressed? *Ambio* 18:112–118.

Firth, P., and S. G. Fisher, eds. 1991. *Global climate change and freshwater ecosystems.* New York: Springer-Verlag.

Firth, P., and G. Wyngaard. 1993. Limnology support at the National Science Foundation. *Bulletin of the Ecological Society of America* 74:170–175.

Francko, D. A., and R. G. Wetzel. 1983. *To quench our thirst.* Ann Arbor: University of Michigan Press.

Gallaher, M. M., J. L. Herndon, L. J. Nims, C. R. Sterling, D. J. Grabowski, and H. F. Hull. 1989. *Cryptosporidiosis* and surface water. *American Journal of Public Health* 79: 39–42.

General Accounting Office. 1991. *Water pollution: More emphasis needed on prevention in EPA's efforts to protect groundwater.* Washington, D.C.: U.S. General Accounting Office.

Gleick, P. H. ed. 1993. *Water in crisis.* New York: Oxford University Press.

Goldman, C. R. 1993. The conservation of two large lakes: Tahoe and Baikal. *Verhandlungen Internationale Vereinigung für Theoretische und Angewandte Limnologie* 25:388–391.

Goodrich, J. A., B. W. Lykins Jr., and R. M. Clark. 1991. Drinking water from agriculturally contaminated groundwater. *Journal of Environmental Quality* 20:707–717.

Gore, A. 1992. *Earth in the balance: Ecology and the human spirit.* Boston: Houghton Mifflin.

Gramp, K. M., A. H. Tpich, and S. D. Nelson, eds. 1992. *Federal funding of environmental research and development.* Publication no. AAAS 92-48F. Washington, D.C.: American Association for the Advancement of Science.

Gregory, S. V., F. J. Swanson, W. A. McKee, and K. W. Cummins. 1991. An ecosystem perspective of riparian zones. *BioScience* 41:540–551.

Grover, B., and D. Howarth. 1991. Evolving international collaborative arrangements for water supply and sanitation. *Water International* 16:145–152.

Gurtz, M. E. 1994. Design of biological components of the National Water Quality Assessment (NAWQA) Program. In *Biological monitoring of aquatic systems,* edited by S. L. Loeb and A. Spacie, 323–354. Ann Arbor, Mich: Lewis.

Hairston, N. G. Jr., and B. T. DeStasio Jr. 1988. Rate of evolution slowed by a dormant propagule pool. *Nature* 336:329–242.

Hall, C. A. S. 1988. An assessment of several of the historically most influential theoretical models used in ecology and of the data provided in their support. *Ecological Modelling* 43:5–31.

Hammer, D., ed. 1989 *Constructed wetlands for wastewater treatment: Municipal, industrial, and agricultural.* Chelsea, Mich: Lewis.

Hart, D. D., R. A. Merz, S. J. Genovese, and B. D. Clark. 1991. Feeding postures of suspension-feeding larval black flies: The conflicting demands of drag and food acquisition. *Oecologia* 85:457–463.

Harte, J., C. Holdren, R. Schneider, and C. Shirley. 1991. *Toxics A to Z: A guide to everyday pollution hazards.* Berkeley: University of California Press.

Hesse, L. W., J. C. Schmulbach, J. M. Carr, K. D. Keenlyne, D. G. Unkenholz, J. W. Robinson, and G. E. Mestl. 1989. Missouri River fishery resources in relation to past, present, and future status. In *Proceedings of the International Large Rivers Symposium,* edited by D. P. Dodge, 352–371. Special Publication of Fisheries and Aquatic Sciences no. 106. Ottawa, Canada: Department of Fisheries and Oceans.

Hilborn, R. 1987. Living with uncertainty in resource management. *North American Journal of Fisheries Management* 7:1–5.

———. 1992. Hatcheries and the future of salmon in the Northwest. *Fisheries* 17:5–8.

Hirsch, R. M., W. M. Alley, and W. G. Wilber. 1988. *Concepts for a National Water-Quality Assessment Program.* Circular no. 1021, Denver: U.S. Geological Survey.

Howarth, R. W. 1991. Comparative responses of aquatic ecosystems to toxic chemical stress. In *Comparative analyses of ecosystems: Patterns, mechanisms, and theories,* edited by J. Cole, G. Lovett, and S. Findlay, 169–195. New York: Springer-Verlag.

Howarth, R. W., R. Marino, R Garritt, and D. Sherman. 1992. Ecosystem respiration and organic carbon processing in a large, tidally influenced river: The Hudson river. *Biogeochemistry* 16:83–102.

Hrbacek, J., M. Dvorakova, V. Korinek, and L. Prochazkova. 1961. Demonstration of the effect of the fish stock on the species composition of zooplankton and the intensity of metabolism of the whole plankton assemblage. *Verhandlungen Internationale Vereinigung für Theoretische und Angewandte Limnologie* 14:192–195.

Hunt, C. E. 1988. *The impact of federal water projects and policies on biological diversity.* Washington, D.C.: Island Press.

Imberger, J., and J. C. Patterson. 1979. A dynamic reservoir simulation model—DYRESM. In *Transport models for inland and coastal waters,* edited by H. B. Fischer, 31–361. New York: Academic Press.

———. 1990. Physical limnology. *Advances in Applied Mechanics* 27:303–475.

Jacobson, J. L., S. W. Jacobson, and H. E. B. Humphrey. 1990. Effects of *in utero* exposure to polychlorinated biphenyls and related contaminants on cognitive functioning in young children. *Journal of Pediatrics* 116:38–45.

Jaworski, N. A. 1981. Sources of nutrients and the scale of eutrophication problems in estuaries. In *Estuaries and nutrients,* edited by B. J. Neilson and L. E. Cronin, 83–111. Totowa, N.J.: Humana.

Jellison, R., and J. M. Melack. 1993. Meromixis in hypersaline Mono Lake, California. 1. Stratification and vertical mixing during the onset, persistence, and breakdown of meromixis. *Limnology and Oceanography* 38:1008–1019.

Jenkins, R. E., and N. M. Burkhead. 1993. *The freshwater fishes of Virginia.* Bethesda, Md.: American Fisheries Society.

Johnston, C. A. 1991a. Sediment and nutrient retention by freshwater wetlands: effects on surface water quality. *Critical Reviews in Environmental Control* 21:491–565.

———. 1991b. GIS technology in ecological research. In vol. 2 of *Encyclopedia of earth system science,* 329–346. San Diego: Academic Press.

———. 1993. Mechanisms of wetland–water quality interaction. In *Constructed wetlands for wastewater treatment,* edited by G. A. Moshiri, 293–299. Chelsea, Mich.: Lewis.

Johnston, C. A., G. D. Bubenzer, G. B. Lee, F. W. Madison, and J. R. McHenry. 1984. Nutrient trapping by sediment deposition in a seasonally flooded lakeside wetland. *Journal for Environmental Quality* 13:283–290.

Johnston, C. A., N. E. Detenbeck, and G. J. Niemi. 1990. The cumulative effect of wetlands on stream water quality and quantity: A landscape approach. *Biogeochemistry* 10:105–141.

Karieva, P. M., J. G. Kingsolver, and R. B. Huey, eds. 1993. *Biotic interactions and global change.* Sunderland, Mass.: Sinauer.

Karr, J. R. 1991. Biological integrity: A long-neglected aspect of water resource management. *Ecological Applications* 1:66–84.

———. 1993. Defining and assessing ecological integrity: Beyond water quality. *Environmental Toxicology and Chemistry* 12:1521–1531.

Karr, J. R., L. A. Toth, and D. R. Dudley. 1985. Fish communities of midwestern rivers: A history of degradation. *BioScience* 35:90–95.

Kitchell, J. F., ed. 1992. *Food web management: A case study of Lake Mendota.* New York: Springer-Verlag.

Kratz, T. K., B. J. Benson, E. R. Blood, G. L. Cunningham, and R. A. Dahlgren. 1991. The influence of landscape position on temporal variability in four North American ecosystems. *American Naturalist* 138:355–378.

Lee, K. N. 1993. *Compass and gyroscope: Integrating science and politics for the environment.* Washington, D.C.: Island Press.

Lee, R. G. 1992. Ecologically effective social organization as a requirement for sustaining watershed ecosystems. In *Watershed management: Balancing sustainability and environmental change,* edited by R. J. Naiman, 73–90. New York: Springer-Verlag.

Lehman, J. T. 1991. Causes and consequences of cladoceran dynamics in Lake Michigan: Implications of species invasions by *Bythotrephes. Journal of Great Lakes Research* 17:437–445.

Lehman, J. T., ed. 1986. *Basic issues in Great Lakes research.* Special Report no. 12. Ann Arbor: University of Michigan, Great Lakes Research Division.

Levin, S. A., ed. 1993. Forum: Perspectives on sustainability. *Ecological Applications* 3:545–589.

Likens, G. E. 1992. *The ecosystem approach: Its use and abuse.* Oldendorf/Luhe, Germany: Ecology Institute.

Likens, G. E., F. H. Bormann, and N. M. Johnson. 1972. Acid rain. *Environment* 14:33–40.

Lillehammer, A., and S. J. Saltveit, eds. 1984. *Regulated rivers.* Oslo, Norway: Oslo University Press.

Lindberg, S., P. M. Stokes, and E. Goldberg. 1987. Group report: Mercury. Chap. 2 in *Occurrence and pathways of lead, mercury, cadium and arsenic in the environment: SCOPE 31,* edited by T. C. Hutchison and K. M. Meema, 17–33. Chichester, England: Wiley.

Lubchenco, J., A. M. Olson, L. B. Brubaker, S. R. Carpenter, M. M. Holland, S. P. Hubbell, S. A. Levin, J. A. MacMahon, P. A. Matson, J. M. Melillo, H. A. Mooney, C. H. Peterson, H. R. Pulliam, L. A. Real, P. J. Regal, and P. G. Risser. 1991. The sustainable biosphere initiative: An ecological research agenda. *Ecology* 72:371–412.

Ludwig, D., R. Hilborn, and C. Walters. 1993. Uncertainty, resource exploitation, and conservation: Lessons from history. *Science* 260:36.

Ludyanskiy, M. L., D. McDonald, and D. MacNeill. 1993. Impact of the zebra mussel, a bivalve invader. *BioScience* 43:533–544.

L'vovich, M. I., and G. F. White. 1990. Use and transformation of water systems. In *The Earth as transformed by human action: Global and regional changes in the biosphere over the past 300 years,* edited by B. L. Turner II, W. C. Clark, R. W. Kates, J. F. Richards, J. T. Mathews, and W. B. Meyer, 235–252. Cambridge: Cambridge University Press.

McDonnell, M. J., and S. T. A. Pickett, eds. 1993. *Humans as components of ecosystems.* New York: Springer-Verlag.

Magnuson, J. J. 1978. Ecological approaches to hydraulic structures. In *Proceedings of the International Symposium on the Environmental Effects of Hydraulic Engineering Works,* 11–28. Knoxville, Tenn.

Magnuson, J. J., B. J. Benson, and A. S. McLain. 1995. Insights on species richness and turnover from Long-Term Ecological Research: Fishes in north temperate lakes. *American Zoologist.* In press.

Magnuson, J. J., H. A. Regier, W. J. Christie, and W. C. Sonzogni. 1980. To rehabilitate and restore Great Lakes ecosystems. In *The recovery process in damaged ecosystems,* edited by J. Cairns Jr., 95–112. Ann Arbor, Mich.: Ann Arbor Science.

Master, L. 1990. The imperiled status of North American aquatic animals. *Biodiversity Network News* 3:1–2,7–8.

Meffe, G. K. 1992. Techno-arrogance and halfway technologies: Salmon hatcheries on the Pacific Coast of North America. *Conservation Biology* 6:350–354.

Melack, J. M. 1992. Reciprocal interactions among lakes, large rivers, and climate. In *Global climate change and freshwater ecosystems,* edited by P. Firth and S. G. Fisher, 68–87. New York: Springer-Verlag.

Miller, T. J., L. B. Crowder, J. A. Rice, and E. A. Marschall. 1988. Larval size and recruitment mechanisms in fishes: Toward a conceptual framework. *Canadian Journal of Fisheries and Aquatic Sciences* 45:1657–1670.

Miller, R. R., J. D. Williams, and J. E. Williams. 1989. Extinctions of North American fishes during the past century. *Fisheries* 14:22–38.

Mills, E. L., J. H. Leach, J. T. Carlton, and C. L. Secor. 1993. Exotic species in the Great Lakes: A history of biotic crises and anthropogenic introductions. *Journal of Great Lakes Research* 19:1–54.

Minckley, W. L., and J. E. Deacon, eds. 1991. *Battle against extinction: Native fish management in the American West.* Tucson: University of Arizona Press.

Moody, D. W. 1990. Groundwater contamination in the United States. *Journal of Soil and Water Conservation* 45:170–179.

Moyle, P. B. 1986. Fish introductions into North America: Patterns and ecological impact. In *Biological invasions of North America and Hawaii,* edited by H. A. Mooney and J. A. Drake, 27–43. New York: Springer-Verlag.

Moyle, P. B., and R. A. Leidy. 1992. Loss of biodiversity in aquatic ecosystems: Evidence from fish faunas. In *Conservation biology: The theory and practice of nature conservation, preservation, and management,* edited by P. L. Fiedler and S. K. Jain, 127–169. New York: Chapman and Hall.

Myers, N. 1993. Tapping into water tables. *Nature* 366:419.

Naiman, R. J., ed. 1992. *Watershed management: Balancing sustainability and environmental change.* New York: Springer-Verlag.

Naiman, R. J., and H. Décamps, eds. 1990. *The ecology and management of aquatic-terrestrial ecotones.* Man and the Biosphere Series no. 4. Paris: UNESCO; Carnforth, England: Parthenon.

Naiman, R. J., H. Décamps, C. A. Johnston, and J. Pastor. 1988. The potential importance of boundaries to fluvial ecosystems. *Journal of the North American Benthological Society* 7:289–306.

Naiman, R. J., H. Décamps, and M. Pollock. 1993. The role of riparian corridors in maintaining regional biodiversity. *Ecological Applications* 3:209–212.

Nash, L. 1993. Water quality and health. In *Water in crisis: A guide to the world's freshwater resources,* edited by P. H. Gleick, 25–39. New York: Oxford University Press.

National Research Council. 1987. *The Mono Basin ecosystem: Effects of changing lake level.* Washington, D.C.: National Academy Press.

———. 1991. *Opportunities in the hydrologic sciences.* Washington, D.C.: National Academy Press.

———. 1992. *Restoration of aquatic ecosystems: Science, technology, and the public.* Washington, D.C.: National Academy Press.

Nehlsen, W., J. E. Williams, and J. A. Lichatowich. 1991. Pacific salmon at the crossroads: Stocks at risk from California, Oregon, Idaho, and Washington. *Fisheries* 16:4–21.

Nemerow, N. L. 1991. *Stream, lake, estuary, and ocean pollution.* New York: Van Nostrand Reinhold.

Nielsen, E. G., and L. K. Lee. 1987. *The magnitude and costs of groundwater contamination from agricultural chemicals.* Agricultural Economic Report no. 576, U.S. of Agriculture Resources and Technology Division, Economic Research Service. Washington, D.C.: Government Printing Office.

Nixon, S. W. 1981. Remineralization and nutrient cycling in coastal marine ecosystems. In *Estuaries and nutrients,* edited by B. J. Neilson and L. E. Cronin, 111–138. Totowa, NJ: Humana.

Nixon, S. W., C. A. Oviatt, J. Frithsen, and B. Sullivan. 1986. Nutrients and the productivity of estuarine and coastal marine ecosystems. *Journal of the Limnological Society of South Africa* 12:43–71.

Nixon, S. W., and M. E. Q. Pilson. 1983. Nitrogen in estuarine and coastal marine ecosystems. In *Nitrogen in the marine environment,* edited by E. J. Carpenter and D. G. Capone, 565–648. New York: Academic Press.

Oremland, R. 1994. Biogeochemical transformations of selenium in anoxic environments. In *Selenium in the environment,* edited by W. T. Frankenberger and S. Benson, 389–419. Marcel Dekker.

Orians, G. H., G. M. Brown Jr., W. E. Kunin, and J. E. Swierzbinski. 1990. Synthesis and recommendations. In *The preservation and valuation of biological resources,* edited by G. H. Orians, G. M. Brown, Jr., W. E. Kunin, and J. E. Swierzbinski, 282–293. Seattle: University of Washington Press.

Patrick, R. 1992. *Surface water quality: Have the laws been successful?* Princeton, N.J.: Princeton University Press.

Patterson, J. C. 1991. Modelling the effects of motion on primary production in the mixed layer of lakes. *Aquatic Sciences* 53:218–238.

Patterson, J. C., B. R. Allanson, and G. N. Ivey. 1985. A dissolved oxygen budget model for Lake Erie in summer. *Freshwater Biology* 15:683–694.

Patterson, J. C., and P. F. Hamblin. 1988. Thermal simulation of a lake with winter ice cover. *Limnology and Oceanography* 33:323–338.

Patterson, J. C., P. F. Hamblin, and J. Imberger. 1984. Classification and dynamic simulation of the vertical density structure of lakes. *Limnology and Oceanography* 29:845–861.

Peterjohn, W. T., and D. L. Correll. 1984. Nutrient dynamics in an agricultural watershed: Observations on the role of a riparian forest. *Ecology* 65:1466–1475.

Peters, R. H. 1986. The role of prediction in limnology. *Limnology and Oceanography* 31:1143–1159.

Petts, G. E. 1984. *Impounded rivers.* New York: Wiley.

Pickett, S. T. A. 1989. Space-for-time substitution as an alternative to long-term studies. In *Long-term studies in ecology,* edited by G. E. Likens, 110–135. New York: Springer-Verlag.

Pinay, G., H. Décamps, E. Chauvet, and E. Fustec. 1990. Functions of ecotones in fluvial systems. In *The ecology and management of aquatic-terrestrial ecotones,* edited by R. J. Naiman and H. Décamps, 141–169. Paris: UNESCO; Carnforth, England: Parthenon.

Porcella, D. B. 1994. Mercury in the environment: Biogeochemistry. In *Mercury pollution: Integration and synthesis,* edited by C. J. Watras and J. W. Huckabee. Chelsea, Mich: Lewis.

Powledge, F. 1984. The magnificent liquid of life. *National Wildlife* 22: 7–9.

Raven, P. H., M. J. Bean, F. W. Davis, G. P. Eaton, S. G. Haines, J. Hezir, J. B. C. Jackson, C. B. Leinberger, J. Meyer, W. A. Molini, N. R. Morin, L. I. Nevling, G. H. O'Ryan, P. G. Risser, R. J. Robbins, J. M. Savage, R. D. Sparrowe, V. J. Tschinkel, and Q. D. Wheeler. 1993. *Biological survey for the nation.* Washington D.C.: National Academy Press.

Reinert, R. A., B. A. Knuth, M. A. Kamrin, and Q. J. Stober. 1991. Risk assessment, risk management, and fish consumption advisories in the United States. *Fisheries* 16:5–12.

Reisner, M. 1993. *Cadillac desert: The American West and its disappearing water.* New York: Viking Press.

Rice, J. A., T. J. Miller, K. A. Rose, L. B. Crowder, E. A. Marschall, A. S. Trebitz, and D. L. DeAngleis. 1993. Growth rate variation in larval survival: Inferences from an individual-based size-dependent predation model. *Canadian Journal of Fisheries and Aquatic Sciences* 50:133–142.

Schindler, D. W. 1974. Eutrophication and recovery in experimental lakes: Implications for lake management. *Science* 184:897–899.

————. 1977. Evaluation of phosphorus limitation in lakes. *Science* 195:260–262.

————. 1987. Detecting ecosystem response to anthropogenic stress. *Canadian Journal of Fisheries and Aquatic Sciences* 44 supp.:6–25.

Schindler, D. W., K. G. Beaty, E. J. Fee, D. R. Cruikshank, E. R. Debruyn, D. L. Findley, G. A. Linsey, J. A. Shearer, M. P. Stainton, and M. A. Turner. 1990. Effects of climatic warming on lakes of the central boreal forest. *Science* 250:967–970.

Schindler, D. W., K. H. Mills, D. F. Malley, D. D. Findlay, J. A. Shearer, I. J. Davies, M. A. Turner, G. A. Linsey, and D. R. Cruikshank. 1985. Long-term ecosystem stress: The effects of years of experimental acidification on a small lake. *Science* 228:1395–1401.

Schottler, S., and S. J. Eisenreich. 1994. Herbicides in the Great Lakes. *Nature* 28: 2228–2232.

Shapiro, J., V. Lamarra, and M. Lynch. 1975. Biomanipulation: An ecosystem approach to lake restoration. In *Proceedings of the Symposium on Water Quality Management Through Biological Control,* edited by P. L. Brezonik and J. L. Fox, 85–96. Gainesville: University Press of Florida.

Sioli, H. 1975. Tropical rivers as expressions of their terrestrial environments. In *Tropical ecological systems: Trends in terrestrial and aquatic research,* edited by F. B. Golley and E. Medina, 275–288. New York: Springer-Verlag.

Smith, J. B. 1991. The potential impacts of climate change on the Great Lakes. *Bulletin of the American Meteorological Society* 72:21–28.

Spencer, C. N., B. R. McClelland, and J. A. Stanford. 1991. Shrimp stocking, salmon collapse, and eagle displacement. *BioScience* 41:14–21.

Sprules, W. G., H. P. Riessen, and E. H. Jin. 1990. Dynamics of the *Bythotrephes* invasion of the St. Lawrence Great Lakes. *Journal of Great Lakes Research* 16:346–351.

Stanford, J. A. 1993. *Instream flows to assist the recovery of endangered fishes of the upper Colorado River basin: Review and synthesis of ecological information, issues, methods, and rationale.* Report prepared for the Instream Flow Subcommittee of the Recovery Implementation Program for Endangered Fish Species of the Upper Colorado River Basin and U.S. Fish and Wildlife Service, Denver, Colorado. Open File Report no. 130–93. Polson: University of Montana, Flathead Lake Biological Station.

Stanford, J. A., and A. P. Covich, eds. 1988. Community structure and function in temperate and tropical streams. *Journal of the North American Benthological Society* 7:261–529.

Stanford, J. A., B. K. Ellis, D. W. Chess, J. A. Craft, and G. C. Poole. 1992. Monitoring water quality in Flathead Lake, Montana: *1992 progress report.* Open File Report no. 128–92. Polson: University of Montana, Flathead Lake Biological Station.

Stanford, J. A., and J. V. Ward. 1988. The hyporheic habitat of river ecosystems. *Nature* 335:64–66.

————. 1992a. Management of aquatic resources in large catchments: Recognizing interactions between ecosystem connectivity and environmental disturbance. In *Watershed management: Balancing sustainability and environmental change,* edited by R. J. Naiman, 91–124. New York: Springer Verlag.

―――. 1992b Emergent properties of ground water ecology: Conference conclusions and recommendations for research and management. In *Proceedings of the First International Conference on Ground Water Ecology,* edited by J. A. Stanford and J. Simons, 409–415 Bethesda, Md.: American Water Resources Association.

―――. 1993. An ecosystem perspective of alluvial rivers: connectivity and the hyporheic corridor. *Journal of the North American Benthological Society* 12:48–60.

Statzner, B., J. A. Gore, and V. H. Resh. 1988. Hydraulic stream ecology: observed patterns and potential applications. *Journal of the North American Benthological Society* 7:307–360.

Sterner, R. W. 1994. Elemental stoichiometry of species in ecosystems. In *Linking species and ecosystems,* edited by C. Jones and J. Lawton. New York: Chapman and Hall.

Sterner, R. W., J. J. Elser, and D. O. Hessen. 1992. Stoichiometric relationships among producers and consumers in food webs. *Biogeochemistry* 17:49–67.

Stouder, D., P. A. Bisson, and R. J. Naiman. 1995. *Pacific salmon and their ecosystems: Status and trends.* New York: Chapman and Hall.

Swift, B. L. 1984. Status of riparian ecosystems in the United States. *Water Resource Bulletin* 20:223–228.

Systematics Agenda 2000. 1994. *Systematics Agenda 2000: Charting the biosphere.* New York: Systematics Agenda.

Terrene Institute. 1993. *Proceedings of the Technical Workshop on Sediments, Corvallis, Oregon, February 3–7, 1992.* Washington, D.C.: Terrene Institute.

Thorton, K. W., D. E. Hyatt, and C. B. Chapman, eds. 1993. *Environmental monitoring and assessment program guide.* EPA/620/R-93-012. Research Triangle Park, N.C.: U.S. Environmental Protection Agency, Office of Research and Development, Environment Monitoring and Assessment Program, EMAP Center.

Tiedje, J., R. K. Colwell, Y. Grossman, R. E. Hodson, R. E. Lenski, R. N. Mack, and P. J. Regal. 1989. The planned introduction of genetically engineered organisms: Ecological considerations and recommendations. *Ecology* 70:297–315.

Triska, F. J., V. C. Kennedy, R. J. Avanzino, G. W. Zellweger, and K. E. Bencala. 1989. Retention and transport of nutrients in a third-order stream in northwestern California: Hyporheic processes. *Ecology* 70:1893–1905.

Turner, R. E., and N. N. Rabalais. 1991. Changes in Mississippi River water quality this century. *BioScience* 41:140–147.

Turner II, B. L., W. C. Clark, R. W. Kates, J. F. Richards, J. T. Mathews, and W. B. Meyer, eds. 1990. *The earth as transformed by human action: Global and regional changes in the biosphere over the past 300 years.* Cambridge: Cambridge University Press.

Vallentyne, J. R. 1974. *The algal bowl: Lakes and man.* Miscellaneous Publication no. 22. Ottawa: Dept. of the Environment, Fisheries, and Marine Service.

Vannote, R. L., G. W. Minshall, K. W. Cummins, J. R. Sedell, and C. E. Cushing. 1980. The river continuum concept. *Canadian Journal of Fisheries and Aquatic Sciences* 37:130–137.

Wake, D. B. 1991. Declining amphibian populations. *Science* 253:860.

Walters, C. J. 1986. *Adaptive management of renewable resources.* New York: Macmillan.

Ward, J. V., and J. A. Stanford. 1982. Thermal responses in the evolutionary ecology of aquatic insects. *Annual Review of Entomology* 27:97–117.

————. 1991. Research directions in stream ecology. In *Advances in ecology: Research trends,* edited by J. Menon, 121–132. Trivadrum, India: Council of Scientific Research Integration.

————, eds. 1979. *The ecology of regulated streams.* New York: Plenum Press.

Warner, R. R., and P. L. Chesson. 1985. Coexistence mediated by recruitment fluctuations: A field guide to the storage effect. *American Naturalist* 125:769–787.

Water Environment Federation. 1992. *Water Quality 2000 final report : A national agenda for the 21st century.* Publication no. TT02. Alexandria, Va.: Water Environment Federation.

Watras, C. J., N. S. Bloom, W.F. Fitzgerald, J. P. Hurley, D. B. Krabbenhoft, R. G. Rada, and J. G. Wiener. 1991. Mercury in temperate lakes: A mechanistic field study. *Verhandlungen Internationale Vereinigung für Theoretische und Angewandte Limnologie* 24:2199.

Webster, K. E., A. D. Newell, L. A. Baker, and P. L. Brezonik. 1990. Climatically induced rapid acidification of a softwater seepage lake. *Nature* 347:374–376.

Wetzel, R. G. 1983. *Limnology.* Philadelphia, Pa.: Saunders.

Wetzel, R. G., T. S. Bianchi, and P. G. Hatcher. 1995. Ultraviolet-B photolysis of dissolved organic matter and enhanced bacterial productivity in aquatic ecosystems. *Environmental Science and Technology.* In press.

Williams, J. E., J. E. Johnson, D. A. Hendrickson, S. Contreras-Balderas, J. D. Williams, M. Navarro-Mendoza, D. E. McCallister, and J. E. Deacon. 1989. Fishes of North America: endangered, threatened, or of special concern. *Fisheries* 14:2–20.

Williams, W. D. 1987. Salinization of lakes and streams: An important environmental hazard. *Ambio* 16:180–185.

————, ed. 1981. Inland salt lakes. *Hydrobiologia* 81/82:i–ix, 1–444.

Wootton, J. T., and M. E. Power. 1993. Productivity, consumers, and the structure of a river food chain. *Proceedings of the National Academy of Science* 90:1384–1387.

World Commission on Environment and Development. 1987. *Our common future.* New York: Oxford University Press.

World Resources Institute. 1990. *Directory of country environmental studies: An annotated bibliography of environmental and natural resource profiles and assessments.* Washington, D.C.: World Resources Institute, Center for International Development and Environment.

Glossary of Terms and Acronyms

ACE. U.S. Army Corps of Engineers

Acid deposition. A form of air pollution caused by NO_2 and SO_2 combining with water vapor in the atmosphere to form nitric and sulfuric acids. This term encompasses both acid precipitation (wet deposition) and the fallout of dry particles containing salts of nitrogen and sulfur.

Adaptive management. "An approach to natural resource policy that embodies a simple imperative: policies are experiments; *learn from them.* . . . Adaptive management takes uncertainty seriously, treating interventions in natural systems as experimental probes" (Lee 1993). Adaptive management is more sharply honed than simple trial-and-error learning because it plans for unanticipated outcomes by collecting and evaluating information. Results from adaptive management reduce uncertainty in the expected outcomes of human interaction with nature (cf. **predictive management**).

Advection. Transport by an established current system in a water body. Advection is considered the mean component of transport as opposed to the fluctuating component, as would be found in dispersive or turbulent flows. Although most advective flows cause horizontal transport, **upwelling** is an example of vertical advection.

Advective processes. Any process that causes **advection.** Examples include wind-driven currents, gyres, upwellings, and gravitationally driven flows such as would be induced by horizontal differences in density structure from nonuniform heating within a lake.

Anoxia. Absence of oxygen in water.

Aquifer. A geologic formation, group of formations, or part of a formation that yields water.

ARS. U.S. Department of Agriculture's Agricultural Research Service.

Biogeochemical cycles. Cycling of chemicals such as carbon, oxygen, phosphorus, nitrogen, and water within or between ecosystems and throughout the biosphere. These compounds are assimilated and broken down over and over again by living organisms.

Biological diversity. The number and relative abundance of different species, the number and type of habitats existing in a particular area, or the heterogeneity of biotic processes. Diversity is a measure of an ecosystem's complexity.

Biological impoverishment. A systematic reduction in the ability to support living systems. Causes can include loss of structural or functional attributes characteristic of a particular environment, including normal variability. Biological impoverishment can take the form of contamination of water resources, extinction of species, destruction and fragmentation of habitat, or reduction of human cultural diversity.

Biophysical patches. Localized diversity of conditions within an ecosystem; smaller areas that are recognized by differences in one or more physical characteristics.

Biotic succession. Temporal changes in the community inhabiting an **ecosystem.** These changes can be driven by physical changes, such as the springtime onset of thermal stratification in a water body, which changes irradiance and nutrient supply; by chemical changes, such as depletion of certain nutrients; or by biological processes, such as colonization of wetlands first by low brush, then by trees.

BMP. Best management practices.

Boundary layer. For fluids flowing near an interface (fluid-fluid or fluid-solid), the thin layer where the flow is influenced by friction at interface. Boundary layers are found in the lowest part of the atmosphere, adjacent to the land and the sea; at the uppermost parts of water bodies; and near the sediment-water interface in streams, rivers, lakes, and oceans (cf. **boundary layer fluid mechanics**).

Boundary layer fluid mechanics. Study of fluid flows in **boundary layers.** Viscous, **shear,** and frictional forces are all important and affect the type of flow present. Forces and velocities within a water body vary in space and time, creating a nonuniform environment for organisms living in it. Flows in the uppermost part of the upper mixed layer, in the **hypolimnion** near the sediment-water interface, and in streams are subject to these forces.

Bounded conflict. Political conflict over environmental policy that is bounded by legitimate restraint, such as a shared commitment to address important issues through continuing debate (Lee 1993). Such conflict over environmental policy is necessary to detect errors and force corrections, but unbounded conflict destroys the long-term cooperation that is essential to **sustainability.**

Cyanobacteria. Formerly called blue-green algae and classified in the plant kingdom, these forms are now classified as a phylum of the kingdom Monera. They photosynthesize as do plants but are structurally similar to other photosynthetic bacteria.

Diel variations. Changes within a twenty-four-hour period, often produced by daily changes in temperature, light intensity, and humidity.

Disturbance regimes. The natural range and distribution of events that cause abrupt and often unpredictable changes in a local environment (for example, floods, wind storms, and disease), changing the habitat for the original organisms and facilitating colonization by new species.

DOA. U.S. Department of Agriculture (also USDA)

DOC. U.S. Deparment of Commerce

DOD. U.S. Department of Defense

DOE. U.S. Department of Energy

DOE NERP. Department of Energy National Environmental Research Park

DOI. U.S. Department of Interior

DYRESM. Dynamic Reservoir Simulation Model

Ecology. A branch of biology that studies relationships among organisms and between organisms and their environment.

Ecosystem. A biological community together with the physical and chemical environment with which it interacts.

Ecotone. Originally indicating the transition zone between plant communities but more recently taken to include transitions between ecological systems of diverse types and spatial scales. These areas are relatively rich in species, containing representatives from each contiguous community as well as edge specialists.

EMAP. Environmental Protection Agency's Environmental Monitoring and Assessment Program.

EPA. Environmental Protection Agency

Epilimnion. In a thermally stratified lake, the layer of water that extends from the surface to the **metalimnion** (cf. **hypolimnion, thermocline**). This layer is analogous to the upper mixed layer in oceanographic terminology. It has smaller gradients in temperature than does the metalimnion. Depending on surface forcing, part or all of the layer may be turbulent.

Estuary. A river mouth subject to effects of sea tides and having a mixture of fresh water and salt water.

Eutrophication. A process in which the nutrient supply of a lake is increased. The input of nutrients (e.g. phosphorus and nitrogen) to lakes varies over a wide range. Several categories are recognized: eutrophic ("well-nourished") lakes have relatively large inputs of nutrients, oligotrophic ("poorly-nourished"), small inputs, and mesotrophic lakes are intermediate. Eutrophication is usually accompanied by a group of secondary changes including higher rates of productivity, an anoxic hypolimnion, and greater abundance of organisms, especially planktonic **Cyanobacteria.**

Evapotranspiration. Loss of water from soil through direct evaporation into the atmosphere as well as through transpiration of water by plants.

Exotic species. A species that is not native to an area, often introduced through human action, but that has been naturalized to the point of being self-sustaining.

Floodplain. That portion of a river valley adjacent to the river channel that is covered with water when the river overflows its banks at flood stage.

Flow regime. Types and patterns of flow occurring in a water body. For example, flow in lakes can be turbulent or **advective,** with some types of advective flow more common near shore, and others more common in the **pelagic zone.** Large lakes with complex geometries are likely to have more types of flow than do shallow, sheltered lakes.

Flow stabilization. Engineered structures and procedures (e.g., dams, flood channels, and levees) that reduce the extent and unpredictability of normal variation in stream or river flow and consequent interference with human activity and infrastructure (for example, agriculture, roads, and buildings).

Fresh water. Water neither salty nor bitter and chemically suitable for human consumption.

Fresh water has a low content of dissolved salts (less than 0.2 percent) and dissolved solids (less than 1 g/L).

Freshwater imperative (FWI). The obligation of policy makers, freshwater scientists, and managers to address the changes in distribution, abundance, and quality of water and freshwater resources that represent an immediate and strategic threat to the quality of human life, the environmental **sustainability** of the biosphere, and the viability of human cultures.

FS. USDA Forest Service

FNS. U.S. Fish and Wildlife Service

GIS. Geographic information system. A combination of computer hardware and CAD (computer-aided design) software that digitally stores geographic information (for example, zoning boundaries, road types, stream sizes and locations, vegetative characteristics, and elevation of landforms), allowing quantitative analyses to be performed on spatial data.

Groundwater. Subsurface water stored in a saturated zone in geologic strata.

Groundwater flow field. Subsurface zone wherein the speed and direction of **groundwater** movement through subsurface pathways are driven by gradients in water pressure.

Habitat. The area where a plant or animal normally lives, usually characterized by either physical features (for example, stream riffle, lakeshore, or submerged wood) or dominant plants.

Heavy metals. Metallic elements that are required for plant and animal nutrition but that become toxic at high concentrations (for example, copper, mercury, cadmium, and lead).

Hydrologic flow path. The path or route that water follows as it moves under all the forces acting on it (gravity, surrounding water pressure, constraint from channel walls, etc.). The flow path may include segments, such as **upwelling** from a spring, surface runoff, downstream river flow, and lake and oceanic currents.

Hydrologic regime. The characteristic behavior of water flow in a drainage basin over a period, based on conditions of channels, water and sediment discharge, precipitation, **evapotranspiration,** subsurface physical characteristics, and so forth.

Hydrology. Study of the occurrence, circulation, and distribution of waters (including precipitation, evaporation, transpiration, surface stream flow, and **groundwater**), with emphasis on their chemical and physical properties and their interaction with their environments.

Hypolimnion. In a thermally stratified lake, the layer of water below the **metalimnion** and extending to the bottom of the lake; temperatures in the hypolimnion are less stratified than in the metalimnion and may approach uniformity (cf. **epilimnion, themocline**).

Hyporheos. The zone defined by penetration of river water into subterranean areas within the active channel and laterally and vertically through floodplain substrata. Water, solutes, and organic and inorganic materials, including uniquely adapted biota, move through large-scale interstitial pathways created by the dynamic nature of floodplain geomorphology.

Indicators. Specific features of a natural system that reflect its condition and that change measurably in response to variations in the system's health, integrity, or **trophic structure.** Indicators may be a certain species or group of species or a composite index of a range of community, trophic, or habitat conditions (see Karr 1991).

Infrastructure. Facilities, equipment, research sites, funding and review programs, and avenues of education and communication needed for freshwater research and management to function.

Interstitial flow. The flow of water in pore spaces within a soil or substrate.

Legacies. Physical remnants, or "signatures," of past disturbances in the form of persistent features of biological communities or their physical environments (for example, changes in distribution or occurrence of plant or animal species) that can be traced to a single cause (for example, habitat alteration or introduction of an **exotic** species).

Limnology. Study of lakes, ponds, rivers, streams, and other inland water bodies as environmental systems. Emphasis can be placed on physics, chemistry, biology, or geology as individual components, but the goal is to understand the components as an integrated system.

Littoral zone. The shallow, near-shore region of a water body, often defined as the band from zero depth to the outer edge of rooted plants.

Metalimnion. In a thermally stratified lake, a layer of water below the **epilimnion** occupied by the **thermocline.** The metalimnion is characterized by a sharp change in temperature or density with depth.

NAPAP. National Acid Precipitation Assessment Program

NASA. National Aeronautics and Space Administration

NASQAN. U.S. Geological Survey's National Stream Quality Accounting Network

NAWQA. U.S. Geological Survey's National Water Quality Assessment Program

NBS. National Biological Service

NGO. Non-governmental organization

NOAA. National Oceanographic and Atmospheric Administration

NPS. National Park Service

NSF. National Science Foundation

NSF LTER. The National Science Foundation's Long-Term Ecological Research Program.

Nutrient cycling. *See under* **Biogeochemical cycles.**

Nutrient spiraling concept. Combined process of resource cycling and downslope or downstream transport. A nutrient atom or organic molecule may pass through the same **trophic** level or chemical state (cycling) during its residence in a stream, but completion of the cycle involves some downstream displacement before the cycle is closed (spiraling).

Organic loading. The mass or quantity of organic material entering a water body, equaling the volume of incoming water multiplied by the concentration of organic material in it. Organic load is normally expressed as a function of the area contributing to the water volume and organic matter concentrations (for example, kilograms per hectare or grams per square meter).

Pelagic zone. The area of an open lake or wetland not including waters adjacent to land.

Population biology. Study of population levels, fluctuations, and distributions and the environmental factors that influence them.

Predictive management. A flexible, proactive technique for resource management based on quantitative estimates of uncertainty. Predictive management seeks to synthesize experience over large spatial and temporal scales and diverse ecosystem types to anticipate and prepare for future surprises (cf. **adaptive management**).

Primary production. Also known as autotrophic production. The creation of organic matter by photosynthetic and chemosynthetic organisms. Primary production ultimately is stored in an ecological community or group of communities (cf. **secondary production**).

Reset mechanisms. Disturbances that set an area or system back to an earlier successional stage (cf. **biotic succession**).

Riparian corridor. The stream channel and that portion of the terrestrial landscape from the high-water mark toward the uplands where vegetation may be influenced by elevated water tables or flooding and by the soils' ability to hold water. It is the interface between terrestrial and aquatic systems that encompasses sharp environmental gradients, ecological processes, and communities. Riparian corridors are an unusually diverse mosaic of landforms, communities, and environments within the larger landscape.

River continuum concept. The idea that a continuous gradient of physical conditions exists from headwaters to mouths of rivers and that structural and functional characteristics of the river's biological communities are adapted to conform to their most probable position or mean state in the physical system (Vannote et al. 1980).

Secondary production. Also known as heterotrophic production. The creation of organic matter by organisms that cannot produce their own food but that consume organic matter produced by plants or present in other living or decaying organisms (cf. **primary production**).

Shear stress. A force that tends to cause parts of a body to slide relative to each other in a direction parallel to their plane of contact.

Sustainability. In this book, *sustainability* is used in the sense proposed by the World Commission on Environment and Development (1987): "The ability to meet the needs of the present generation without compromising the ability of future generations to meet their needs."

Thermocline (planar). In thermally stratified lakes, the horizontal plane or surface of maximum change of temperature with respect to depth. It is contained in the **metalimnion.** Diurnal thermoclines are created by the alternation of heating and cooling and wind mixing over a day and may be transient; the seasonal thermocline is a more persistent feature.

TVA. Tennessee Valley Authority

Toxicants. Poisonous substances or agents, especially those used to kill rather than repel pests.

Trophic structure. Energy flow of an ecosystem as illustrated by feeding relationships in food chains and food webs (see also **trophodynamics**).

Trophodynamics. Movement and transformation of food energy and nutrients in food webs.

Turbidity. Cloudy condition of water caused by suspended and dissolved solids.

Upwelling. Rising of water toward the surface from subsurface layers in a body of water (opposite of sinking).

USDA. U.S. Department of Agriculture

USGS. U.S. Geological Survey

Watershed. A ridge of high land dividing two areas drained by different river systems; also the region or drainage basin draining into a river, river system, or body of water.

Water table. The surface of an unconfined groundwater body, defining the top of the saturated zone.

Wetlands. Those areas inundated or saturated by surface water or **groundwater** at a frequency and duration that are sufficient to support, and that under normal circumstances do support, a prevalence of vegetation typically adapted for life in saturated soil conditions.

Xenobiotic. A foreign (allochthonous) organic chemical, especially an environmental pollutant such as a pesticide in runoff water.

About the Authors

ROBERT J. NAIMAN received his Ph.D. from Arizona State University in 1974. He is currently the director of the University of Washington's Center for Streamside Studies, which focuses research and education efforts on riparian management in the Pacific Northwest. His own research efforts include the ecological dynamics of streams and rivers, the role of large animals in influencing ecosystems and landscape processes, and riparian processes. He is actively involved with UNESCO's Man and the Biosphere (MAB) Programme and is chair of the U.S. MAB Program's Temporate Ecosystems Directorate.

JOHN J. MAGNUSON serves as professor of zoology and director of the Center for Limnology at the University of Wisconsin-Madison and principal investigator of the North Temperate Lakes Long-Term Ecological Research Site. He earned his BSc and his MS from the University of Minnesota in fisheries science and his Ph.D. in zoology from University of British Columbia, Canada. His research interests are in fish and fisheries ecology, long-term ecological research on lake ecosystems, including climate change effects, and comparative analyses across diverse ecosystems.

DIANE M. McKNIGHT received a Ph.D. in environmental engineering from MIT in 1979. Since then she has been a research hydrologist with the U.S. Geological Survey–Water Resources Division. Her interests are in biogeochemical processes involving trace metals and natural organic material in freshwater ecosystems. Current research focuses on acid mine drainage-streams in the Colorado Rocky Mountains, glacial meltwater streams in the McMurdo Dry Valleys, Antarctica, and wetlands at the Rocky Flats nuclear facility, near Denver.

JACK A. STANFORD is Jessie M. Bierman Professor of Ecology at the University of Montana and is also director of the Flathead Lake Biological Station. He received his Ph.D. in limnology from the University of Utah in 1975, and has studied lakes and streams throughout the world, and in particular, the Flathead River-Lake ecosystem in Montana and British Columbia. Current research projects include landscape ecology of floodplains of gravel-bed rivers, emphasizing the role of interstital flow and groundwater upwelling on biotic diversity and productivity; influences of environmental change on the mass transfer of materials and pelagic primary productivity of the oligotrophic Flathead River-Lake ecosystem; and biophysical factors controlling the longitudinal distribution, abundance, and growth of biota in large rivers and lakes, with emphasis on the ecology of endangered fishes. Professor Stanford has served on or chaired many scientific review panels and is well known internationally for his scientific synthesis of environmental issues.

Index